# The  ZOZO PHENOMENON

*Darren Evans and the original "Zozo board."*

*The back of the Zozo board. Credit: John Weaver, used with permission.*

# The Zozo Phenomenon

Darren Evans and Rosemary Ellen Guiley

Visionary Living, Inc.
New Milford, Connecticut

*The Zozo Phenomenon*


By Darren Evans  and Rosemary Ellen Guiley

Cover design by Jacob Evans
Frontispiece illustrations copyright John Weaver. Used with permission.
Back jacket and interior design by Leslie McAllister

ISBN: 978-1-942157-02-1 (pbk)
ISBN: 978-1-942157-03-8 (e-pub)


Published by Visionary Living, Inc.
New Milford, Connecticut
www.visionaryliving.com

# Acknowledgments

The stories featured in this book are published with permission, and many of them contain sensitive personal information. With a few exceptions, we have used pseudonyms in order to protect privacy. We have used generic terms such as "spirit board" and "talking board" in most instances, since many boards are not the trademarked Ouija versions, and Zozo activity is not limited to any particular type of board. We would like to thank all those who have submitted stories, and who have granted us permission to share them.

We would also like to thank John Zaffis, Karen A. Dahlman, Robert Murch, Josh Allen, and Marion Nobu for their contributions to this book; Jacob Evans for his design of the front cover; and John Weaver for his illustrations of Darren Evans and the original "Zozo board."

Darren has a special thanks for Stephen Lancaster, Mary Ellen Evans, Tonya Potts, Brittany Ervin, and Vera Kuzminova.

# Table of Contents

# Foreword
# by John Zaffis

Zozo is a powerful negative entity that likes to attack people who use a spirit board. It has other ways of attacking people, but its recent track record shows that it prefers the board. People who run into Zozo have unhappy stories to tell. They suffer nightmares, all kinds of unpleasant paranormal phenomena, have all kinds of breakdowns in daily life, and, in some cases, experience forms of oppression and possession.

When I say "recent," I mean within the last forty or so years. In my work investigating cases of bad hauntings and demonic interference, I started encountering Zozo in the 1980s, at about the time when a lot of people starting having Zozo experiences, too. Nobody realized how global these cases were until one Zozo victim, Darren Evans, began a one-man "demon hunt" to find out exactly what was going on.

For Darren, it has been a tough, uphill battle, because whenever you shine a light on anything that lives in darkness, it strikes back.

There are many reasons why Zozo has surfaced all over the planet, as you will discover from the excellent and thorough research done by Darren and Rosemary Ellen Guiley, one of the leading experts in the paranormal field. Like me, Rosemary has spent several decades doing field investigations of all kinds of hauntings, including those involving negative beings and spirits.

Zozo may seem like a recent player, but this entity has a long, long history that probably reaches into ancient times. Dark entities love to shapeshift, and it seems this one has found its current favorite tactic of striking through a spirit board. Unlike other kinds of spirit communication tools, millions of spirit boards are readily available, and they are easy to use.

Most activities involving a spirit board, or Ouija board, are neutral. Just because you use a board does not mean you are going to have problems, or encounter Zozo. But plenty of people do, unexpectedly.

Many of them have never heard of Zozo until he announces himself by pointing to the letter Z, or spelling out his dominant name, ZOZO.

I consider the spirit board to be neutral myself, but I recognize that many people get themselves into difficulty by using one, and so I do not recommend them. There are quite a few reasons why people run into trouble. This book is a riveting examination of one of the biggest troublemakers of them all, and the factors that contribute to his ability to pester people.

Darren tells his own shocking story, from the day his life changed when he innocently learned of a strange spirit board buried beneath a house and began to use it. His life turned upside down, and literally "went to hell" as Zozo gained power. An important part of Darren's healing was to turn around and confront this entity, and then to uncover its secrets and make them known to others. It has not been easy for him. We may never know all the secrets, for, as I mentioned, entities like to shapeshift to keep people off guard. One very important point about *The Zozo Phenomenon* is that the information in it will raise awareness so that those kinds of hide-and-seek tactics are harder to carry out.

Rosemary has done a great deal of research on negative entities, including demons and the Djinn, and has had her own run-ins with them, as she has documented in some of her many books. In addition, she has done extensive research on spirit boards and the dynamics of what happens when people use them. She, too, has had encounters with Zozo.

In the second part of the book, Rosemary and Darren combine their research to examine Zozo and his origins, history, and behavior. They also have advice to help others avoid problems or resolve them.

The book is full of the true stories of those who have met Zozo and suffered for it. People from all over the world have poured out their hearts to Darren when they have learned they are not alone. In the forty-plus years that I have been investigating in the paranormal, I am no stranger to extreme cases, and I find that many of these accounts fall into that category. Perhaps the most alarming part is, they are only a fraction of the total number of accounts that Darren has collected.

Darren and Rosemary also pay important attention to the human side of the picture as well, examining the factors that contribute to vulnerability when people use spirit boards. In dealing with the dark side, we cannot ignore the human element. What people do, feel, and think, and what is happening to them in daily life, affects their experiences when they open the door to the spirit world. This applies to all cases of negative entity contact regardless of whether or not spirit boards have been used. Many of these cases are complicated with no easy solutions.

In addition, we have to be especially aware of the influence of the media and the entertainment industry, which have "demonized" spirit boards for decades. As a result, many people mistakenly believe that all spirit boards are "bad."

I do not use a spirit board myself. I avoid them and do not recommend them. But I also recognize that they are neutral. They do not guarantee that anything, good or bad, will happen. The users determine that with what they bring to the board.

*The Zozo Phenomenon* is a ground-breaking book of great value to all in the paranormal field, and to the public as well, for many of the Zozo victims are not involved in paranormal work or investigations, but are casual board users. For the first time, this book puts a spotlight on an entity that plagues untold numbers of people. It educates people about spirit board use. I have always said that information and knowledge are some of our best defenses against negative entities, in whatever way they choose to strike out.

# Introduction
## by Rosemary Ellen Guiley

How does an entity like Zozo manage to insert itself into so many spirit board sessions? One answer may be our very collective attitude toward the board itself.

The spirit board is one of many spirit communication devices, but it, more than any other tool, it has acquired an aura of mystery, and even a tinge of darkness and danger, especially about its origins. In fact, spirit boards began as simple commercial ventures, made by the manufacturers of toys and novelties, with no other purpose than to be appealing and entertaining to consumers, and in return, to make a profit. There was nothing conspiratorial or sinister behind the conception and development of spirit boards, including the Ouija. Today, thanks largely to Hollywood horror films and misinformation passed around consumer and paranormal circles, many people think the board itself is "bad" or "evil," but that is not the case. Amazingly, all kinds of people with little or even no experience on the board condemn it.

As an interface between worlds, the spirit board is neutral—neither good nor evil. The experiences that people have with a board depend on them and how they use it. Everyone brings something to a board experience: thoughts, intentions, fears, anxieties, desires. All of those factors contribute to the nature of the experience, and even whether or not there is any experience at all.

People can and do have negative experiences, even when they do not expect them, as many of the stories in this book illustrate. There are negative entities that look for all kinds of opportunities, and the high level of usage of spirit boards provides many openings.

The branded Ouija has been around for more than a century. Devices similar to the Ouija are much older. In earlier times, contact with spirits and the gods was performed by oracles and priestly castes, people who had marked mediumistic skills and training. Today, thanks to the availability of many devices and tools, anyone can become an oracle, and without the benefit of study or training. That's where much of the problem lies, for the average person is unprepared to deal with the quirky and sometime problematic nature of the spirit world—and especially with troublesome and negative spirits that find their way through.

The Ouija was born in the late nineteenth century as a combination of two popular spirit communication devices, a dial plate, in which words were spelled out on a lettered dial, and the planchette, a platform with a pencil that enabled handwritten messages to be communicated by spirits through a user's hand. Businessmen who made novelty toys saw commercial potential, and secured a patent for the "Ouija" in 1891.

Initial sales were brisk, due to the high level of popular interest in Spiritualism and spirit communications via mediumship. The original Ouija company, Kennard Novelty Company, underwent changes and reorganizations. It became The Ouija Novelty Company under the direction of William Fuld, who moved aggressively to squash competition. Fuld formed the William Fuld Manufacturing Company. By 1919, he had acquired all outstanding rights to the Ouija, thus consolidating his power.

The years from 1919 to 1926 were intense and busy for Fuld, who filed more trademarks and patents. He even trademarked the term WE-JA to protect the pronunciation of "Ouija." He launched a second line of cheaper boards, the Egyptian Luck and the Hindu Luck, to thwart competition, and also launched a line of Ouija jewelry and even a Ouija oil for the treatment of rheumatism.

In February 1927, Fuld suffered a fatal accident. He liked to do a lot of his own repairs at his manufacturing plants, and went up on the roof of his three-story building in Baltimore to repair a flagpole. His support gave way and he fell, catching himself on a window, and then plummeting to the ground. Amazingly, he suffered only a concussion and a few small broken bones. En route to the hospital, his luck changed. A broken rib pierced his heart and he died later that day.

In 1966 the Fuld family sold William Fuld, Inc. and all of its assets to the game and toy manufacturer, Parker Brothers. General Mills acquired Parker Brothers in 1968, and then merged it with a subsidiary, Kenner, in 1985, creating the Kenner Parker Toys, Inc. Tonka acquired the company in 1987. Both Tonka and Parker Brothers were bought by Hasbro, Inc. in 1991.

The patent on talking boards expired in 1908, allowing anyone to create one, although exact copies of the Ouija are illegal. The name "Ouija" and "The Mystifying Oracle" are still under trademark.

Over time, the board shrank in size, and changed composition. The original boards were wooden, then masonite, a hardboard made of wood fibers compressed by steam and pressure. Masonite is a tough material that does not burn easily, and thus gave rise to the legends that boards would not burn because they had "evil" spirits attached. Today's boards are made of cardboard.

The Ouija and other talking boards were considered forms of entertainment in their early decades. Plenty of people got themselves into trouble, however, by listening to bad advice imparted by alleged spirit communicators. Many of those cases involved wish fulfillment— the users had predispositions to desired answers and used the board for permission to carry out undesirable behavior and wicked deeds, including murder.

Hollywood quickly discovered the appeal of using the Ouija in horror films, in which evil spirits are contacted by naïve users, then jump the board and create mayhem. Of all the films featuring talking boards, *The Exorcist* (1973) and *Witchboard* (1986) had the greatest influence in persuading people that bad things—possession and murder—will happen if a spirit board is used. Subsequent films have reinforced the stereotype.

## The origins of "Ouija"

Fuld liked to cloak his talking board in mystery and mystique, and was vague about how the board acquired its name. According to one explanation, the name is the combination of French and German words for "yes." A board named "yes yes" doesn't make much sense, however, when the board is designed to offer "yes" and "no" answers.

The board evidently named itself. Two of the original men who created the board, Charles Kennard of the Kennard Novelty Company and Elijah Bond, the patent holder, were stumped for a name and decided to ask the board directly. Also present at this session were Bond's wife and son, and, most importantly, his sister-in-law, Helen Peters, who was quite mediumistic. When asked for its name, the board spelled out OUIJA and said it meant "good luck." At the time, Peters was wearing a locket that showed a figure of a woman and the word 'Ouija' across the top of it. She said she had not thought of this word for the name during the session. The men liked it and decided to adopt it.

## Bad spirits and talking boards

Even though spirit communication tools are neutral, negative experiences are possible. Opening the door to the spirit realm does not guarantee a good experience. Entities of all types and dispositions are capable of seizing the opportunity to communicate, and the more unwary and inexperienced the people are, the more vulnerable they may be to predatory spirits. Those who have studied the spirit world and understand how to deal with it know how to dismiss pesky and dangerous spirits, but others do not. Especially vulnerable are teens and young people, who are easily conditioned by the media, and may even want a scary experience in order to impress their friends.

There are plenty of hostile entities glad to oblige.

It should be no surprise that a manipulative entity like Zozo has been able to rise in presence and prominence over the past several decades. The proliferation of millions of talking boards and eager human communicators provide plenty of opportunities for enterprising predators to make contact with potential victims. The rise in the "demonization" of the board predisposes many users, even subconsciously, to anticipate a negative experience. As accounts in this book demonstrate, Zozo makes use of other spirit communications tools as well, but the talking board seems to be a favored one.

## Working on *The Zozo Phenomenon*

Whenever I undertake research or work on the dark side of the paranormal, I experience a host of phenomena ranging from baffling to irritating to problematic. Upon starting *The Zozo Phenomenon*, I girded myself for the onslaught of "the usual." These are a few of the things that disrupted the work:

- Emails concerning the book that never arrived or went missing after arrival
- Document files that went missing or became corrupted
- Computer malfunctions and shutdowns

- Audio recordings that became corrupted
- Interference on phone calls, including dropped calls, static, yowling, and other line noises
- Mechanical malfunctions at home, chiefly, a garage door that kept going up and down by itself
- Increased sightings of shadow figures
- Innumerable disruptions of daily life that went beyond explanation or "coincidence"

As annoying as these phenomena were, they pale in comparison to the terrors described by victims in this book. Entities like Zozo are real, and the experiences that people have with them are genuine. By putting the spotlight on Zozo, Darren Evans and I are seeking to raise awareness and educate, so that others can avoid becoming victims.

In this book, we examine the different aspects of Zozo, its history, possible explanations, and bizarre associations. We also discuss the factors behind Zozo experiences, warning signs, and how board users can better protect themselves from any kind of negative encounter.

# Part I
# Darren's Story

Darren Evans recounts his dark odyssey from the day he discovered a mysterious talking board emblazoned with the name ZOZO. Along the way were upsetting events, freak outs, breakdowns—and then the unsettling realization that he was not alone in his contact with Zozo.

# 1

## The Dark Side of the Board

The bizarre Ouija board looked ominous. Found underneath my girlfriend's house, it was unlike anything I had ever seen. It was wooden and old, but unlike the traditional Ouija, it was double sided. The back side had been handcrafted for a mysterious purpose.

The front side bore the standard vintage William Fuld Ouija design that we later were able to trace back to the 1930s. These old boards were made of wood, larger than boards today, and with squared corners. The back surface—what would soon become known as "the dark side"—chilled me to the bone.

The background was black and a deep shade of gray, painted on top of a smooth polished wood grain. It had a weathered appearance. Strange symbols were engraved upon the dark background, and inlaid with a metallic silver leaf. Long, spidery, tentacle-looking drippings were carved into the surface and filled with black candle wax, which gave the appearance that the dark side was "latched" onto the regular talking board side.

Even stranger than its construction, however, was the peculiar name hand-engraved on the dark side: ZOZO. On each side surrounding this word were bat-like wings. Overall the dark side of the board had a heavy, fiendish look.

The dark side appeared to have burn marks on each corner, and was well abraded, suggesting that someone had used this board frequently or over a long period of time.

I had not seen the term "Zozo" before, but, as a fan of classic rock music, I was familiar with something similar: the term "Zoso," which Jimmy Page, the lead guitarist for Led Zeppelin, had used on the band's fourth album, featuring the hit song *Stairway to Heaven*. In fact, all of the band members had signed the album with their own occult-looking symbol. Page's symbol of Zoso had been adapted from a symbol found in an old magical text.

The "Zozo" term made me immediately fascinated by this mysterious, double-sided board.

## The beginning of my encounter with evil

The year of the discovery of the "Zozo Witch Board," as I called it, was 1982. I had no idea what lay before me: a growing obsession with playing with the board, and an entanglement with a hostile entity that latched on to me and would not let go. If I had had any inkling of the future, I would have run as far away as possible from that board. But I didn't, and now I am telling my grim story in the hopes that others will not repeat it.

My girlfriend at the time, Jamie, was a beautiful young lady whose family lived directly across from my grandma on the west side of Tulsa, Oklahoma, near the banks of the Arkansas River. Jamie was as mysterious as she was beautiful, with auburn hair and emerald green eyes that shined like a cat under a silver moon.

Jamie and I were not the ones who discovered the double-sided board that hot August day. A plumber found it while working underneath the house and handed it over to Jamie's father, Joe, who was not pleased. Joe declared that Ouija boards were nothing to mess around with. I was so fascinated by it that his words bounced off me.

I crawled underneath the house to where the board had been found, and to my surprise, there were more objects in the spot. In a circle surrounding the area where the Zozo board had been found were old lightning jars, so-called because of the embossed lightning on the sides.

They had metal clasps holding the glass lid with levers to clamp it down on the rubber seals. The jars were wedged into the hardened earth, and I had difficulty pulling them out.

On the outside of these vintage jars was a white, pasty substance. I could not see what was inside. I wiped away some of the white stuff with a towel, and held the jar up to the sun. I almost dropped the jar in shock. I was staring into the blood filled eyes of a dead blackbird! I found four jars, one for each corner of the Ouija, and each one contained a fully preserved blackbird. I never quite understood why these feathered friends were accompanying the double-sided spirit board, but one can imagine my surprise when, two decades later, I discovered that one of the definitions for the word "zozo" is *blackbird* or *crow* in the ancient Basque language!

I also did not understand at the time that for centuries blackbirds have been associated with omens of misfortune and also predictions of the future. Were they put into these jars as a warning?

Jamie's parents believed in spirits and ghosts. I had already been told by both Joe and Jamie's mother, Tara, that the house was haunted. I agreed. I had once witnessed a door open all by itself, which was creepy, because shag carpeting made the door difficult to pull open by hand.

Joe called the ghost "Leonard," and commented that it had followed him around for years. Joe instructed Jamie and me not to ever make Leonard angry. We were also told to leave the strange Ouija board alone, because we were not experienced in the spirit realm. Tara was a self-professed Wiccan, and was much more comfortable with the spirit world. She told us stories of fairies and other paranormal creatures on late nights when I was allowed to sleep over.

Tara was the kindest of souls, but not one to underestimate! She collected all kinds of books on witchcraft and astrology. Jamie and I were inseparable, and would spend hours and hours discussing things that go bump in the night. Finally, curiosity got the better of us, and we decided to sneak out the double-sided board, which was stored in a purple "spirit cloth." I wondered in the back of my mind if it wasn't Joe who had constructed this wicked-looking object, as he was an expert Indian silversmith who often made jewelry in his shop. He was the only one that I could imagine having the know-how to make such a work of art.

Jamie had elected not to go on a family trip to Branson, Missouri, so that we could spend Friday and Saturday night together alone. I sneaked out of Grandma's house and joined her for a few beers at her house while she played her favorite songs on the radio. Sometimes I would play the guitar while she would sing. Up until that night, our relationship was full of puppy love and innocence. That was about to change.

I was irresistibly drawn to the mysterious Ouija board. Despite its dark appearance on the reverse side, I wanted to explore the whole mystery of the Ouija. Jamie was just as curious. She sneaked into her dad's room and found it on a shelf in the closet. I will never forget the look in her eyes as she walked up and sat it on the kitchen table.

"Which side should we play on?" she asked with a devilish grin.

I had fashioned a planchette-style centerpiece from a Def Leppard cassette tape, and set it next to the Ouija. The room was dark, and Jamie had lit one of her mom's many candles. We decided to try the regular side first. We set up the homemade planchette and placed our hands gently on it.

Almost immediately it scurried around the board on its own. I was amazed, because I knew I was *not* moving it! Was Jamie? She assured me she was not, and I believed her because of the way the pointer scooted very quickly off the board and onto the table, where it stopped just short of the edge on Jamie's side. I placed the plastic piece back onto the board.

"Let's try again," I said hastily.

This time, the pointer traced a large figure eight pattern, swiftly moving in a very deliberate manner. I asked whose board it was, and it continued its circular movement and then abruptly stopped on the letter L. Then it inched to E, O, N, A, R, D—the name of the resident ghost!

"Holy shit, Jamie, it spelled Leonard!" I exclaimed. I could feel the adrenaline suddenly coursing through my body.

I was astonished. We were having a conversation with a real ghost! We gathered our senses and again placed our fingers on the plastic when *bam bam*! we heard a loud knock on the front door. We both jumped as if we were watching a scary film at the midnight movies. We hesitated and then walked into the living room and approached the front door.

"Who is it?" Jamie asked.

No one answered. Jamie yelled, "Who is there?"

Again silence.

My heart beating in my chest, I flung open the door.

Nobody was there. I stepped out onto the front porch and looked up and down the street. Nothing. To say that this added a creep factor to our first Ouija session is an understatement.

I looked at Jamie and she was white as linen. I tried to rationalize what was going on, and consoled my girlfriend as best as I could.

"Someone is joking around," I offered lamely.

Jamie's eyes looked huge and watery. She was holding back tears of fear. I hugged her tight and we decided to put up the board for the night. She made me sneak the double-sided Zozo board back into her father's room, and we cuddled up on the couch and tried to sleep. I could feel her heart beating through our embrace.

Thirty minutes or so later, we were almost asleep when *bam bam*! another series of knocks bellowed from the front door!

Jamie and I jumped up and nearly took off running to the opposite end of the house. Then I heard "Darren!" It was a voice I knew— my best friend Randy. I opened the door and there was a welcome face. We had talked the day before, and I had forgotten that I had invited him over. He arrived smelling of beer, and offered me one. I gladly accepted.

Jamie asked Randy if he had knocked on the door earlier, and he said no. His car was in the driveway, and he said he had just left a party on Coyote Trail, a good fifteen miles from Jamie's house. We told him about our Ouija experience, and Randy was determined to join the excitement.

Randy reminded me of the comedian Chris Farley of *Saturday Night Live!* fame. Large, in charge, and funny as all get out. He loved the Australian band ACDC, and he suggested we try to contact the band's deceased lead singer, Bon Scott. Randy idolized the hard-partying vocalist, and mimicked his thirst for wine, women, and song. Randy's favorite ACDC song was *Highway to Hell*, a song that later proved ironic when my best friend took his final road trip and abruptly lost his life.

I felt better about using the board with Randy around. Jamie kissed me goodnight, and went to bed. I went into Joe's room and retrieved the board from the closet. I brought it back into the kitchen, where Randy was chugging another beer, and set it on the table. Randy stared at the double-sided board and was mesmerized.

"Holy shit, bro!" he said with gusto.

We placed our fingers lightly on the plastic piece and Randy demanded that we speak to the spirit of Bon Scott. The planchette moved more slowly than the first time, and it made spirals again. Suddenly it spelled AYE MATE. We laughed at this unusual response. It was using an Australian expression! Randy was transfixed. We continued a conversation for about twenty minutes, and then the board requested Randy to roll a joint. We were convinced that the communicator was really Bon!

Randy twisted a joint. Then he heated a fork over the gas stove until it was red hot, and stabbed the plastic homemade planchette to make a hole. He lit the joint and took a few puffs and then poked it into the hole.

An incredible thing happened: the cherry glowed like someone was taking a hit! I couldn't believe my eyes, but Randy was convinced he was partying with his rock and roll idol. We enjoyed more conversation until suddenly the centerpiece spelled SEE YOU IN HELL. Randy laughed out loud at the chilling statement, taking it as a joke. I did not share his enthusiasm.

## The end of Randy

That session haunted me twenty years later when Randy and I used a Ouija board for old times' sake in Oklahoma City. During the session, Zozo came on and said Randy was cursed, and taunted him with an evil precision. Although it had been twenty years, Randy maintained his dark sense of humor and began to cuss the entity. Again, the board spelled out SEE YOU IN HELL.

I asked if we had really been talking to Bon Scott on that summer night long ago in Tulsa. The answer was HAHAHAHA. The communicator revealed that it had been Zozo the entire time. Randy asked how he was going to die, and it spelled "KAR WRECK AT NIGHT ALONE. "Car" was misspelled with a "k."

A year after this ominous premonition, I was auditioning for a band in Oklahoma City. Randy kept calling me and sending me text messages asking me to call him. I couldn't answer right away because it was loud at the rehearsal studio, and I was among many people auditioning. I performed two songs and was jubilant when, at the end of the session, I was asked to join the band.

On the way home, I had a message on my cell phone from Randy. He sounded upset and depressed. I listened to him ramble on for about five minutes as he cried and said he didn't know if he could go on. There was something peculiar about the way he was carrying on in the voice message. He told me that he loved me, as if he were saying goodbye. Randy had recently been treated for depression and had been prescribed medications. I arrived home in Oklahoma City worried about my best friend. We were about as close as friends could be.

I called Randy back and he answered the phone.

I said, "You okay, man?"

There was an uncomfortable pause. Then all he said was, "Darren... I will see you in *hell*." He hung up.

I called back and the call went straight to voice mail. Randy had turned off his phone.

I went to sleep that night very concerned. His words were etched into my mind—and still are to this day.

The next morning, I was at work in Midwest City, Oklahoma, when the phone rang. It was Randy's girlfriend, Gloria. She was crying and sobbing. The hairs on my neck stood straight up and a chill ran up and down my spine.

"Randy's *gone*, Darren!"

"What do you mean, he's gone, Gloria?" I responded.

"He's dead, Darren!"

My eyes swelled with tears. *My best friend was gone!* I could hardly believe it.

Gloria went on to tell me that Randy had consumed a fifth of vodka and then crashed her SUV into a telephone pole less than a mile from their residence. I had been the last person to talk to him alive.

I had never felt such a wave of sorrow. I went outside and punched a brick wall. My blood and tears fell to the concrete. I took a three-day leave to grieve Randy's death. I went home and sat in my music studio and played ACDC at full volume and cried until I could not cry any more.

I cannot say with certainty that our experiences with the Ouija played a role in Randy's untimely death, but the foreboding predictions in different sessions twenty years apart were too eerie to dismiss. Randy was always the life of the party. Immense in size as well as popularity, he was adored by his family and long list of friends. There is not a day that goes by that I do not think about my best friend. His life and death continue to have a profound effect on me and anyone who knew him.

## The window incident

After my first few sessions on the double-sided board, I became obsessed with the Ouija. I became the guy who would bring a Ouija over to your house if you did not believe in the spirit world, just to convince you that it did exist. The board always performed, and I was unaware just how much the planchette was propelled by Zozo. In reflection, I wish that double-sided Zozo board had not been found. I began to change.

In 1988, I married Jamie on Halloween. My best man was my friend, Michael. His girlfriend, Trina, was a friend of Jamie's. Trina did not believe in ghosts or spirits. Mike did, and asked me once to come over and bring a spirit board to try to convince her. I considered it a challenge. Soon, much to her dismay, Trina became a believer.

It was a starry summer night when Jamie and I arrived at their house with a spirit board, a chalice, and candles. We were now incorporating the elements of earth, wind, and fire into our sessions, as their inclusion seemed to intensify the séances. We set up at the coffee table in the living room. Jamie lit the candles and I poured soil into the chalice and burned incense. We began a session that would soon turn chaotic.

Immediately the planchette began to move in what was now its usual circular motion, gliding slowly at first, then speeding up as if it were building energy. It spelled out WINDOW. We all looked at the two windows in the living room but noticed nothing. We all looked at each other with nervous anticipation. Again we tried, and again it spelled WINDOW. For twenty minutes or so, that was the only word it would spell.

"There has to be something going on with a window!" Jamie declared.

The planchette then slowed down to a crawl, and formed a large circle repeatedly. We were about to give up on the session when, without warning, the circular movements revved into top gear, and the spirals became tighter and tighter with amazing speed. The planchette jockeyed out of the pattern and abruptly spelled HELLO.

Trina made some sarcastic comments in reference to her skepticism, and Michael asked her to get us all some beers before we continued. She walked across the room towards the kitchen with a sardonic look, shaking her head. She turned the corner and within seconds we were jolted by an intense, terrifying scream, and the sound of broken beer bottles.

"There is someone at the window!" she yelled.

Michael and I locked eyes for a fraction of a second and then bolted out the door to the front yard. A tall man with a bald head and light blue scrubs was running away down the street. We gave chase. Michael and I were in our early twenties, and were quite fast, but this guy was pulling ahead. I noticed his long strides—he had to have been six feet six inches tall! My adrenalin was pumping and my feet were flying. Michael was close behind, screaming obscenities.

We tailed him for two blocks until he ducked down an alley and jumped a fence. The red and blue lights of police cruisers were lighting up the night sky in front of a building where the perpetrator disappeared from view. Out of breath, we yelled out to an officer who was taking a report and told him what had happened. He told us to remain calm and to stand behind his vehicle. He shared our information on a police radio and informed us that the tall man fit the description of the person they were looking for.

The building was a behavioral health center for the mentally challenged. Administrators had called police when the man in question escaped. The freaky-looking peeping Tom went back to his room, where he was questioned by authorities.

Another officer exited the building and joined us to fill out paperwork on the incident. After hearing our version of what happened, both officers went back into the facility to obtain additional information from the suspect, who was now under a lockdown protocol. Michael and I paced the parking lot for about twenty minutes until the officers returned.

One of the officers had a sarcastic smile on his face as he told us they had asked the strange man why he had escaped and was peeping in people's windows. His response was chilling: "The Devil made me do it."

We walked back to Michael's place, buzzing from the night's events. Michael wanted to continue the board session, but his girlfriend did not share his optimistic curiosity. Trina was furious. She had thrown the board outside, and was visibly shaken by the creepy turn of events.

"Keep that fucking thing out of my house!" she shrieked. "It's *evil!*"

That session quickly made a reluctant believer out of Trina, and reinforced Michael's excitement for the dark side. Michael then had a new idea, one we would both soon regret. He implored me to burn the board.

Over the years, I had picked up boards at thrift stores and yard sales, and some of them I had burned as a result of my experiences with them. One particular time I heard hisses and a piercing scream-like sound as the board burned.

Michael grabbed a large gas container from the storage building on the side of the house. I placed the board in the middle of the front yard and heard an unexpected sound. *Church bells* were ringing after midnight! Our eyes met. Why would they be chiming this hour of night? It only added mystery to the disconcerting events that had taken place.

I poured gasoline all over the board, and tossed the near empty gas can to my left towards Michael. He backed away. I had found a book of matches and struck one, pausing before I threw it onto the board. I had a weird feeling. What happened next seemed like slow motion. I tossed the lit match onto the board and it burst into a tall flame. I ran backwards, but to our horror a *trail of fire* ripped out from the board over to the gas can across the yard. The container exploded.

Michael was too close. His upper torso caught on fire, and he screamed in agony. The yard was swiftly engulfed in flames, and Michael rolled frantically around, trying to put out the fire that was burning his arms and chest.

I ran inside and yelled for someone to call 911. Trina was frantic and wailed as she bolted out the door to help Michael. Luckily, he managed to douse the flames on his body, but he was severely burned. Trina put him in their car and sped away to the local emergency room a few miles away across downtown Tulsa.

Jamie had called 911, and in less than ten minutes the fire department, and the same police officers were on the scene. Firefighters used extinguishers to douse the charred front yard and the hedges that were aflame. I had odd thoughts about the Bible and the story of Moses and the burning bush.

The officers were not pleased. They threatened me with several charges before finally calming down, and ordered me to go home and leave these people alone. I felt horrible. I had only done what Michael asked me to do.

Jamie and I decided to head to the hospital to check on my friend, but first I walked over to the spirit board. *It had survived the fire unscathed.*

Michael was not so lucky. He had received numerous burns and was in quite a bit of pain when I caught up with him at the Oklahoma Osteopathic center downtown. Trina looked at me with hate-filled eyes—I could tell she blamed me for everything.

Fortunately, Michael would be okay. After he recovered, he was still obsessed with everything surrounding that night, even though he had gone through hell. Years later, we would get back on a spirit board, and then it had a very sinister message for us all.

## The end of Michael

In 2001, Michael and I ran into each other at a bar in Collinsville, Oklahoma. He was now with his wife, Shelia, and he introduced us. We were shooting pool and having a few beers when the subject of the spirit board came up.

"Come over to the house and let's show Sheila what it will do," Michael said. Sheila smiled in approval.

I made a quick homemade talking board and went to their house. Michael and I joked that we would not be flinging gasoline this time. The session that night was hit and miss, but towards the end of the evening Michael asked how he would die. The centerpiece quickly spelled MURDER.

At the time, I didn't put much stock in this warning.

At the end of that night, we shook hands, and I did not realize that it would be the last time I would ever see my good friend alive. Sheila found her husband in their driveway a few months after this last session. At first she thought he had passed out, but when he would not wake up, she called 911. My close friend and best man at my wedding was dead.

I did not find out until more than two months later. I will never forget the night I called looking for him while I was out of town. His daughter answered the phone. She broke down and told me her daddy was dead. I asked what had happened. She cried and told me I would have to speak with her mommy. Sheila got on the phone and told me Michael was poisoned. Hearing Sheila break down on the phone triggered a gut-wrenching response from deep within my soul.

I was standing outside in Coffeeville, Kansas, while I listened to this devastating news. I hung up the phone and vomited. The cold wind blew against the tears on my face. My friend was gone.

Michael's death remains unsolved to this day. Sheila was a suspect but was cleared after a long investigation. I ran into Sheila while working at a loan company in 2012. She had an account at the office I where I worked. We embraced and engaged in small talk as I walked her back to her car.

She looked up at me with a tear in her pretty blue eyes. "Michael loved you, Darren," she said.

I told her I loved them both, and how sorry I was that I had been unable to attend Michael's funeral due to an out of town trip.

That was the last time I saw Sheila. In 2015 she was killed in a head-on collision on a highway near her home in Collinsville, Oklahoma.

Randy and Michael died six years apart, but their memories will haunt me for an eternity. I feel somehow to blame for their premature deaths. Maybe if we had not asked how they would die, the course of fate would have changed. I continue to tell others that I highly recommend that people do *not* ask questions regarding death on spirit boards.

Once with Jamie, I had asked the board how I would die. I was told I would be stabbed to death. Now that the board had accurately predicted the demise of two of my friends, I waited with dread for that shoe to drop.

I would have to wait for years.

# 2

# Total Meltdown

The last time I ever used the double-sided Zozo board was in the late 1980s, in a bizarre session in Jennings, Oklahoma with Jamie. I was obsessed with the board and with Zozo, and I was pushing the envelope by demanding Zozo show itself. I asked if it could control my mother-in-law's dog. This generated some laughs to those present during this séance. The laughter however, quickly turned to alarm. It was just the beginning of a crazy chain of events I will never forget.

## The possessed dog

Jamie's mother, Tara, had a Yorkshire terrier mix dog, Sadie, that was in the den way down the hall. I ordered Zozo to make the dog come to me. Unbeknownst to us at the time, the door that separated the den from the hallway leading to the room where we were playing on the board was closed. We heard Sadie scratching on the door down the hall. She was barking and carrying on so much that Tara opened the door. To our amazement, the dog came running up to us and sat down right next to the board, shaking and quivering as if it were afraid. We all looked at each other like WTF!

The dog remained sitting there, shivering. Jamie and I put our fingers back on the planchette, and I ordered Zozo to make further demonstrations of its power. I asked if it could make the dog go back to the den. Suddenly the dog ran off back down the hall and began barking and scratching the door that Tina had closed. I followed to witness its behavior. It was if the animal was indeed being commanded telepathically.

Tina opened the door and asked what the hell was wrong with the dog. I chose not to say that it was being instructed by a demon, as by this time, Tara was against us using the board in her home. We were rebellious teens, and I was engrossed in my obsession with Zozo. This was months after the discovery of the double-sided "Zozo Witch Board," and I had no intentions of refraining from my new addiction.

The dog was now back inside the den. Tara left the door open for the little Yorkie to run back and forth as it saw fit. We ordered it to return, and here it came again with an odd sense of urgency. We never called out to the dog by its name, but Zozo spelled out that it would INVADE SADIE. Despite Sadie running back and forth as ordered, I remained skeptical that a spirit could manifest such a physical response over another life form.

The room then grew quiet and a heaviness could be felt. Sadie trembled more than ever, and began whimpering. Jamie had become frightened as well, and would not partake in any further experiments. Sadie growled and became increasingly agitated. Horrified, we all watched this poor dog as it coughed and wretched up disgusting vomit on the floor where we were sitting. Everyone stood up and Jamie's cousin, Rosalyn, bolted toward the den to tell Tara.

Tara was pissed! She tried to pick up her dog, who snapped at her with sharp teeth and a vicious demeanor completely out of character for the normally docile canine. Sadie was going berserk. When Tara saw the spirit board, she began to cry, and looked up at me with a combination of disgust, frustration, and horror.

Tara grabbed a broom and whisked the little dog out the front door. Sadie bolted awkwardly into the woods, yelping and gagging. The experience left us all confused and frightened. I was given strict instructions to get rid of the board, and if it was ever found back in the house, I would be barred as well. I did what I was told.

I took the Zozo board and walked towards the forest. I was trying to take in the reality of what had happened. While I felt responsible, I also felt invigorated. I had been able to manipulate an animal through some type of mind control. Or, Zozo had been able to do it.

## Camp Ouija

I wandered deep into the wooded area surrounding the property. About two miles in, I stumbled upon an abandoned fortress of sorts. An old bus had been made into a makeshift camper. I was cautious, as I could tell someone had lived here for quite some time. A canopy was erected along the side of the bus, and gave shade to a small wooden picnic table that was weathered and falling apart. A clothesline was pinned between the trees with tattered remains of fabric blowing in the wind.

I looked inside the bus. Immediately I noticed a long barrel rifle standing at attention next to the rusty entrance. Inside, I saw that someone's belongings were scattered about. Old playing cards were spread in solitary fashion on a table. Beer cans spilled out of a trash barrel. Dust covered nearly everything. This place had been sitting here a long time undiscovered. I found a huge album collection and a vintage stereo system. There was a generator, a small stove, and a hot water heater that was wired up. I wondered why someone would be hiding out in the middle of nowhere.

I noticed an old rusty British convertible Austin Healy sports car a short distance away. Whoever left all this stuff had good taste! I decided the trunk would be a good place to stash the dreaded, double-sided Zozo Witch Board. I lifted up the trunk lid, and the hinges played a rusty violin. I placed the board on top of a moldy old blanket. I couldn't bear to just throw it away. It was too elaborate, too ornamental, too powerful. I left it in the sports car and walked back to the house, feeling like I had lost a friend.

By the time I got back, Jamie's house was dark and silent. Everyone had gone to bed. The dog had not returned. I stayed up with mixed emotions. I made myself a cup of coffee, and sat in the living area next to a large picture window. The night breeze was blowing the curtains, like a ghostly slow motion waltz. Abruptly, I heard a howling in the distance. It was Sadie! I slid out the front door and listened. The sound sent waves of chills up and down my skin. Sadie was howling and crying from afar. She sounded evil. I have nightmares of that sinister sound. It was an amalgamation of primal fear and suffering—the sound of madness.

I found Sadie a few days later with her throat eaten out. Something had attacked her, in more ways than one. I cried as I buried her little body. I felt responsible for her death. I was losing control of my actions. A line was blurred between what was right and wrong.

The days following Sadie's tortured demise were not cool, to say the least. I was not on good terms with Jamie or her family after this ordeal. I began a slow drift away from my family, my wife, and myself. It was if I were being pulled by a slow rip-tide towards a lost current of the unknown. I told no one of my discovery of the abandoned site, which I nicknamed "Camp Ouija," and what I had done with the board.

## A growing obsession

Out of sight was not out of mind. I could not get the Zozo board out of my head. The thrill of the board was enticing. I felt powerful while on it. I believed I was on the verge of discovering something supernatural. I was changing. I had to have the board again.

I fought the urge to go back into the woods and retrieve it. After a few weeks, I could not stand it any longer. I woke up one morning and left without letting anyone know where I was heading. I was going to stay at Camp Ouija for a few days and work the board.

I packed a few sandwiches and a thermos of water and off I went. The forests were thick and the leaves were rustling in the Oklahoma autumn. The trek took about an hour. I had a rough time trying to find the camp, and several times I almost turned back. Then I saw a familiar hill, and just beyond it was the isolated camp site. I felt it calling my name. I was impressed by the mystery nomad who had created this hidden existence. I wanted to be like him. I wanted to find another side of myself. A side that was a shadow within. And, like the double-sided Zozo board, I would find myself attached to something dark and disconsolate.

I sat under the canopy and it reminded me of an old western covered wagon. To the east were the remains of an overgrown garden feasted upon by ground ivy and ragwort. Tools were under a lean-to. I felt an odd comfort.

My reverie was interrupted by a scurrying noise that came from the rusting sports car. I looked at it, taking in its flat tires and top that was skewed down. What was making that noise?

I crept within ten feet of the back of the Austin Healy, and again I heard a rustling. It was coming from the trunk! I inched ever closer and paused. Nothing. I could see the crack that separated the trunk lid from the back valance. I lifted the lid upward and all hell broke loose.

Rats of every size literally became airborne, flying out of the trunk and all around me. I nearly shit my pants. I toppled backward and let out a scream that I'm sure scared the rodents as much as they did me!

The trunk lid fell back down to its resting place. I crawled backwards, slapping my neck and head repeatedly as if phantom rats were crawling on me. They scattered as fast as it happened. Suddenly there was silence, except for the sound of my pounding heart. I broke off a long stick and again lifted the trunk, ready to run in case there were more rats inside. I looked inside, and at first I thought the Ouija was gone—or was it? A stinging smell of piss and feces slapped me in the face. The rat pack had devoured the double-sided board! I could make out a tattered mess of the blanket, twigs, leaves, straw, upholstery, and, amazingly, shredded Ouija. I shuddered, imagining a large, aggressive male daddy rat with incredibly long whiskers chewing away at the heavy board!

The thought of demon-possessed rats coming back to their vehicular dungeon was not appealing, so I found an old rim lying next to a farm truck not far from the car. I threw it on top of the trunk. I sat back under the covered awning next to the bus. A bright drop of red blood ran down my chin and jumped off onto my wrist. A twinge of sharp pain stung my mouth. I had bitten my lip during the fracas!

I grabbed my backpack and took a drink from my thermos, the metallic, fishy taste of blood mixing with the liquid. I saw a painted cow skull perched on a tree limb. It seemed to be smiling at me in a menacing grimace. Perhaps Camp Ouija was too much for this city boy.

## Breakdown

Jamie and I slowly drifted apart over the years, in part because of my obsession with the spirit board. I conducted hundreds of sessions on various boards, both store-bought and homemade. The entity Zozo kept saying things like I was a "chosen one" and that it was my guardian angel. It promised to give me powers to control others. It said it was a king of kings, a ruler of realms. I became more and more obsessed with it. I believed a lot of what it was saying, and I wanted more.

I was not disappointed. The original Zozo board was gone, but Zozo the entity was not. Somehow it was able to track me, and communicate on whatever board I used. The deeper I got into Zozo, the more my personality underwent a marked change for the worse.

Jamie divorced me in 1992, and I hit the road chasing hail storms to earn a decent living—if that's what you could call my existence for several years. My life became a string of failures and bad luck. I developed severe anxiety and wound up in various emergency rooms for full-blown panic attacks that would come out of nowhere. The anxiety attacks would start in my hands, causing a tingling, numbing sensation that would build in intensity. The tingling would escalate into a constant electrical sensation that would spread outward from my hands to my arms and down my torso, until I felt like I was being electrocuted. I remember describing the sensation to doctors as like a freight train running though my body. They attributed this odd feeling to oxygen saturation due to hyper-ventilation. I was a mess, and I suspected that I was under some kind of curse or attachment. I had a nervous breakdown in 1993 that left me a broken man.

I suffered hallucinations of people's faces melting off into wicked skeleton-like beasts. I was paranoid and delusional. I showed up on my mother's doorstep, crying and begging her to save me from these faces. Mom says she knew from the moment she looked into my eyes that there was a demon inside me. I collapsed into her arms and she put me in the guest bedroom, where I fell into a deep sleep for twenty-four hours. While I was out, she laid hands on me and performed her own version of an exorcism. Mom was a Rhema Bible School graduate and specialized in healing ministry. She recited passages from her studies and told me that during the deliverance, she saw shadows flying around in circles above me.

When I woke up, I felt like a new man. I'm not sure if it was God, or just the comfort of being in the peaceful presence of my wonderful mother, or both, but I felt amazing the next day. I told myself I would leave the spirit board alone and start going to church. I couldn't believe how different I felt.

I vowed I would stay away from spirit boards—but soon the temptation was back, and, once again, it was impossible to resist.

# 3

# Kill Darren

In 1999 I moved to Michigan and started dating a woman who was very skeptical of ghosts, and simply dismissed spirit boards as a parlor game. Despite my misgivings, I decided to show her what could be done. Marshall was a small town about thirty miles from Battle Creek, and there were no stores that sold spirit boards of any kind, so I downloaded an image of one from the internet. My girlfriend, Liza, rolled her eyes as it printed out on a standard eight by ten sheet of paper.

We taped the paper onto a piece of cardboard, sat down, and put our fingers on a homemade planchette. I asked if there were any spirits present. To Liza's shock, the pointer quickly moved to YES. I asked where the spirit came from. It spelled CYBERSPACE. I asked where it was now, and it spelled SKULL NECKLACE.

Liza chuckled at this revelation. Her son Mickey wore a big skull necklace, a type popular with the teenage skate boarders in the area. Before I could ask anything else, the planchette swooped back and forth between the Z and the O repeatedly. Liza commented that she could definitely tell I was not moving the centerpiece. Her eyes lit up. She was instantly fascinated and wanted to learn more about this Zozo character. I told her I didn't think that was a good idea, and I closed the session immediately. The next day, Liza came home with a brand new glow in the dark Ouija board.

After work, I arrived to find Liza and her nieces crouched down in her bedroom playing on their new toy. They looked up and said that Zozo was super nice, telling them jokes. The two middle school children were laughing and having a ball with this seemingly delightful spirit. I decided to get creative.

I grabbed a notebook and wrote down various colors on separate pieces of paper. I then made sure no one was looking and crunched the papers into little wads and hid them from view. I shuffled the papers so even I did not know which ones were which. I picked one and held it in my fist.

"Ask it what is written down on this paper I am holding," I said.

The pointer spelled SKY BLUE.

I had written the word "blue" on one of the papers, but could it be this one in my hand? I tossed it down onto the board and Liza unfolded it. Sure enough, it was the paper that I had written down the word "blue." Even more amazing, the marker I had used to write down all the colors was labeled SKY blue!

This game continued, and the girls, using the board, were able to correctly identify every color on the papers. We all were beside ourselves in disbelief. I took it a step further.

I grabbed an encyclopedia from the living room and opened it up randomly to a page describing King Arthur. I hid the contents of the book from their view, and asked questions about this historical character. Again, using the board, they answered the questions correctly! I was dumfounded.

Then things got morbid. The planchette began counting the alphabet backwards and then spelled KILL DARREN. I sat down next to the girls to get a better view. The girls giggled and asked if it wanted Darren dead. It spelled YES. They asked why, and it spelled WITH GOD.

I didn't like where this was going. I asked out loud, "Where are you?"

The planchette scooted across the letters to spell MIRROR. I remembered how Zozo would tell me to look for it in mirrors.

Through the years it had often told me I could always find it there. All I ever saw was my own reflection, until now. There was one mirror in Liza's bedroom. It hung on the south wall of the room. All four of us looked up to the mirror, and to our horror we saw Mickey's skull necklace looking right at us all through the reflection. The lighting in the room was dim, but the necklace was swaying back and forth with glowing red eyes. Mickey had hung it on one of the bannisters on Liza's bed the day before. The angle of the reflection from the skull gave the appearance that Zozo was watching us the entire time through the red plastic eyes. The timing of all this was off the charts!

The girls shrieked and we all ran outside, terrified. Liza's nieces cried and demanded to go home. In a few moments this board session had gone from playful to psychic and then to horrific, orchestrated by some crafty intelligence.

Suffice it to say that things did not work out well for me in Michigan. On top of it, I could not get used to the harsh winter.

In 2002 I moved back to Oklahoma and had a beautiful daughter with my new girlfriend, Vera. We named her Kirsten, and in 2004 we moved to Del City, Oklahoma. I don't know what caused me to get back on spirit boards after all the weird experiences I had had, but I started up again.

I had met a cool guy named Jay who was a drummer, and we recorded music in my garage. One night, Jay and I were having a discussion about spirits, and he said he was on the fence about the possibility of contacting them. I told him about some of my board experiences and he just smiled unconvinced. I cracked open a beer and quickly made another homemade talking board from cardboard.

We sat down and concentrated on our intent. It had been a few years since I had played and I did not want anything negative to come through. We decided we would only ask the board fun stuff, so we rested our fingers on the triangle and within a few moments it began moving in large circles.

Jay was quite amazed that it was actually working. "If there are any spirits here, show us a sign," Jay said.

Not five seconds later, a strange thing happened. A huge spider crawled out from under the table and scurried across the board! Jay's eyebrows shot up.

## The iron tongue

Jay and I had discussed forming a music group, and the next question we asked was what our name should be. Without hesitation the triangle spelled IRON TONGUE. This made us both smile. Hmm, Iron Tongue… that sounded pretty hardcore. We both liked that name for a hard metal project. Then something began to make a weird noise just outside the living room window. A strange humming sound—was it the wind?

Vera asked if she could try working the board with me, so I agreed. She swapped seats with Jay and placed her fingers on the centerpiece. Vera said out loud that she didn't like the name Iron Tongue and the board would have to do better than that.

The entity did not respond well to her mocking attitude.

"What is your name?" she asked.

ZOZOZOZOZO spelled over and over, getting faster and faster. Then things got ugly fast.

YOUR DAUGHTER WILL HAVE IRON TONGUE the board spelled with a speed that was alarming. I had had enough, and I ended the session.

Jay went home, and I ripped up the homemade board and threw it in the trash outside.

Hours later, I woke up from a nap and went to the bathroom, and my heart almost stopped at what I saw. My two-year-old daughter was drowning in the bathtub! Her nose was the only thing sticking out of the water and she was struggling, arms flailing about. In an instant, I grabbed her out of the tub. She coughed up water. My heart was pounding. How did this happen?

Kirsten had somehow left her bedroom and crawled into the tub and turned on the water. If I had not reached her when I did, I believe she could have died.

We got her settled down, and she did not appear to need any medical attention. That would all change within twenty-four hours.

I got a call from Vera at work the following day, saying Kirsten had developed a high fever. She said she was taking her to the Midwest Regional Medical center emergency room. I met Vera at the hospital, and Kirsten was quickly admitted. The next two weeks were some of the most agonizing of my life.

Kirsten's high fever alarmed the doctors. I called a pastor of a local church to come pray for my daughter. Kyle Peterson showed up a few hours later and walked into our room where nurses were working with Kirsten. I told Kyle about her condition which was worsening daily, and he began to pray. "Heavenly Father we pray for this girl in the name of Jesus. Let there be no *unclean spirit* in her presence." Pastor Peterson was a big man of African descent. I had seen him preach at his church and I had never witnessed anyone with such fire for the Lord.

A doctor came in during the prayers to check Kirsten's vital signs. In front of Kyle, he reached around her neck and felt something. There was a large tick on the nape of her neck! The doctor found it just a moment after Patterson had asked that no unclean spirit be in her presence. Everyone was amazed at the timing of this odious find. Doctors scrambled to diagnose my daughter's condition. Because of the tick, they tested her for Lyme's disease and Rocky Mountain spotted fever. Both tests were negative.

The medical team placed Kirsten in intensive care and we all were put in isolation. Kirsten was fading away. I overheard two doctors talking about her condition and heard one of them say that she was more dead than alive.

My poor daughter! As the days went by, I cried and cried. Finally, we got the news. Kirsten had MRSA (methicillin-resistant staphylococcus aureus), a dangerous bacterial infection that is resistant to most antibiotics. She had not responded to the two powerful antibiotics she was administered, and doctors told us there was only one left to try. During this ordeal I could not help but wonder if Zozo was responsible in some way. Again, the timing was uncanny.

Kirsten's face became incredibly swollen. Most horrifying, her mouth was the area of the most intense swelling. Her tongue protruded grotesquely from her mouth. It was the worst thing I had ever seen. I couldn't get Zozo's words out of my head: YOUR DAUGHTER WILL HAVE IRON TONGUE.

I had to take off from work to be with my innocent little girl. At times she would look up at Daddy with such sadness and horror in her eyes. Words cannot describe the helplessness we felt. I would never be the same.

As my daughter clung desperately to her life, I remained steadfast and prayed like I had never prayed before. Vera and I never left her bedside except to use the restroom and eat. For two weeks we were in hell. By the grace of God, Kirsten responded to the last round of antibiotic. The swelling subsided. I will never forget when she woke up and asked Mommy if she could have some Kentucky Fried Chicken. My beautiful daughter was going to be okay!

Kirsten is now twelve years old as of this writing, and has no memory of her ordeal. Part of this story was discussed years later on the show *Ghost Adventures: Aftershocks*, and remains the most horrifying series of events I have ever experienced.

But there would be more.

## Disturbances

After leaving the hospital, we tried to get things back to normal at home. Vera moved in her brother Danny to the spare bedroom. One night I woke up hearing voices coming from somewhere in the house. I thought it might have been Danny, but after walking around, I determined that everyone was asleep.

That morning we were eating breakfast, and Danny said he hadn't slept very well the past few nights because he kept hearing voices. He was not scared, but he said he had no doubt the place was haunted.

About a week went by. One day we were all hanging out in the den when we heard and felt a tremendous boom that shook the entire house. I bolted out the front door because I thought a truck had slammed into the house, but nothing was there. The neighbors also heard the huge sound. We checked the roof tops, but nothing could be found that could make such a forceful noise. The violent power of it is hard to describe. It was unlike anything I had ever felt. It remains a mystery what happened that day, but everyone in the house was shaken by it.

We all continued to hear the weird humming noise, which followed us around. The voices also continued and became a regular occurrence. You could not make out was being said. It sounded like twenty to thirty people talking all at the same time. The house was alive with activity.

I walked into the kitchen late one night to get a drink of water and saw a huge snake crawling on the tiled floor. A copperhead! I grabbed a broom and beat the shit out of it. I could not believe how long it took me to kill the damn thing.

After that, I decided I was tired of all the bullshit. I called Pastor Peterson.

Kyle came to my home to do a blessing and brought me some holy oil. He requested that only I join him for the "exorcism" of the house. Kyle walked around silently for a few moments with a fierce look in his eyes. We walked into the garage and he stopped. He turned around and gave me a cold look with his intimidating eyes. "Darren, did you use a spirit board in this garage?"

I was stunned. How did he know? "Yes," I replied, finding it hard to look him in the eye.

"This is where it lives." Kyle began shouting at the top of his lungs. I was startled by his almost violent outburst. He was deadly serious, and continued yelling all through the house for about fifteen minutes before he calmed down and his shouts became whispers. I could feel the atmosphere change. Kyle was a powerful agent of Christ, and after he left so did the voices—at least at this house.

Vera and I were together for almost four years before we went our separate ways. We remain friends and she is a wonderful mother to our daughter Kirsten.

After the hospitalization with our daughter I stopped participating in spirit board séances. Despite that decision, the weird events continued. Zozo told me repeatedly that it would never leave, and for many years it would indeed be there waiting for me. Every time I got on a board there it was, like it had been there the entire time. In many of the Zozo stories shared with me, people report the same thing, that it is always there, and no other spirit entity comes through except it.

## The stabbing comes true

Zozo had predicted two of my close friends' deaths. Again, as I mentioned before, it also predicted that I would die by a stab wound. This grave prediction nearly came true when I was brutally attacked in 2013 by my second wife, Kathleen, with a large kitchen knife on a hot summer evening. We were at my son's apartment in Tulsa. We argued that night and things got pretty physical. I had to hold Kathleen down because she was trying to hurt me. She had admitted to using the spirit board behind my back, and Zozo came through. The scars from that night remain in more ways than one.

I walked out the door to get away from the scene. I went for a walk and returned about thirty minutes later. I had noticed Kathleen's behavior was getting more and more erratic. The front door was locked and I knocked on it. When it opened, I saw a woman possessed.

"*Go die!*" she screamed and lunged at me with a knife, stabbing me in the head and shoulder before I had any chance to react. The next few hours were full of blood and gore.

I screamed for my son to call 911. I held onto my shoulder to apply pressure, but the wound was too deep. Blood spurted into the air and hit the walls. I really thought I was going to die. I had no idea how much blood one could lose and still live, but I was about to find out the hard way. The wound on my head was also spewing blood, and it ran down into my eyes. I could barely see, and I started to feel light headed. Blood was everywhere.

My son, Jacob, reacted swiftly and made a split-second decision to drive me to the hospital, though I feared I was losing too much blood to make it there in time. We walked down the stairs to his car and I left a trail of blood the whole way and into the vehicle.

My daughter, Kirsten, was at the apartment asleep along with Jacob's daughter. Jacob feared that calling 911 would bring the police to the apartment and they would take the children because of the horrific scene. I was now dizzy from the loss of blood, and I told Jacob to take me to a convenience store about a half-mile from his apartment.

When we got to the store, I had enough energy to jump out and burst through the door, yelling for help. There was a line of people inside and they recoiled in shock when they saw my wound squirting hot red blood all over the store. I fell to my knees; I felt the end was near. I saw a woman gag and run out of the store, covering her mouth. The patrons were shocked to see such a sight. Seeing the responses from customers only increased my sensation of nausea. I could not hold back a deep wrenching pressure to vomit, and I hurled violently. The scene was ghastly and chaotic. A man took his shirt off and rushed over to me and applied pressure to my shoulder wound. The white tee-shirt became completely saturated with blood in seconds. He yelled out something in Spanish that I didn't understand. A store clerk called 911 and said an ambulance would be there soon.

I was now lying down in a pool of blood. It reminded me of a gory horror film, only I was not an actor, I was the victim of my own horrific reality show. I was fading away. Thoughts of Zozo's prediction swam in my clouded mind. My vision got blurry and I could not think straight. I thought I was dying. I felt sleepy. People were screaming and running away from the widening pool of blood that was now covering a large portion of the floor. I was still lying in it when the paramedics showed up. I was rushed to Saint Francis Hospital with massive bleeding.

Fortunately, the knife did not cut though any major arteries, though you could never tell by the way blood was pumping out of my body. I was sewed up and sent home a few hours later.

Kathleen was gone. I lied to the police about what had happened. I never filed charges. Even though my wife had stabbed me, something inside me just would not let me do that. I didn't want her to spend twenty years in prison for this. The police were not happy. Investigators finally showed up at my son's apartment looking for Kathleen, but by then she was gone.

The healing process was laborious. The blade had severed muscle tissue in my left shoulder and it would be weeks before I could lift anything. I had internal bleeding that concerned the doctors. A huge blood bruise appeared near the wound site and traveled down into my trunk area and snaked down over time into my left leg. Doctors feared it would clot, and told me to come back to the emergency room if I had stroke symptoms. That was not a comforting thought. Nor was the sight of this traveling hemorrhage. When it seeped its way down my leg, at one point it was in the shape of a letter Z! I wasn't out of the woods quite yet. I must have a pretty hard head, as the wound on my skull wasn't nearly as deep as the flesh wound on my shoulder. I was lucky to be alive.

Zozo was only partially correct about dying by stabbing. I would live to see another day.

# 4

## The Haunted House

I moved my family from Tulsa to Oklahoma City during the summer of 2009. I had located what seemed like a great deal, a four-bedroom, two-story home with a full basement for only six hundred fifty dollars a month! I met the landlords at the property, which was located near downtown. Although it was not in the nicest of areas, I did not have much choice monetarily but to agree to a one-year lease and move in.

The landlords had me meet a maintenance guy there who was cleaning up the place. He was quiet and did not look me in the eyes when we spoke. I was pressed for time and money, so after a quick walk-through, I called the owners and quickly made arrangements for the home. I figured that despite the location, it was big enough for two of my sons, Justin and Jacob, one of their girlfriends, Karlee, my Uncle Tom, and my two-year-old girl, Alison.

My girlfriend was spending time with her mother in Midland Odessa, Texas, and I called her and gave her the news. She planned to join me in a few weeks. I rented a U-Haul and we made the one-hour trip to move our belongings into the home. While we were unloading the heavy bedroom furniture we quickly discovered a huge problem. The stairway leading to the upstairs was unusually thin, and nothing bigger than a coffee table would fit! Why would anyone build such a thin stairwell?

I did not think to ask the maintenance guy how the furniture would be carried upstairs. I was stressed out over the move. Also, why was the old furniture from the previous tenants still in the house? I called the owners to find out the previous family had left suddenly, leaving most of their possessions. They offered no explanation as to their departure. Some of the stuff was nicer than mine. They said we could have it, but that did not set well with me. I still had the problem of carrying our stuff upstairs and figuring out what to do with the former residents' belongings.

Having experience as a contractor served me well. I managed to remove a large picture window from the east side bedroom and hoisted down everything we did not want. Using ladders and ropes, we lifted our beds and dressers up through the opening. I noticed the window had not been removed in the past, and wondered how in the hell they got their stuff up there. I never did find out. This was just the first mystery of this unusual house.

Beside the super skinny stairway was a very narrow kitchen wall. It barely left room to maneuver beside the stove and sink. There was a large boxed-in structure in the odd-shaped living room that was noticeable as soon as you walked through the door. I assumed by its shape—it had a vertical column above the square wooden shape—that it had been built to cover an old wood burning stove. I never understood what it really was, or why it was built there. The floors were definitely not level by any means, and creaked loudly in several areas. During the first few days, we noticed how the ground floor seemed to be leaning towards the old basement. I chose the basement for Alison and I, as it had its own bathroom and a long walk-in hallway closet.

The creaky floors were outdone by the stairs leading to the upper level. Although carpeted, the stairs roared out every time someone walked up or down. I could hear it all the way into the basement. The place made noises everywhere. Whenever someone flushed the toilet upstairs you could hear the gurgling of old pipes belching water through the septic system. It was annoying, to say the least.

The basement stairs were steep and dangerous for my two-year-old, Alison. I purchased baby gates, and she made it a game to figure out ways to overcome her barriers. Alison slept in a crib, and I slept across the room in an electric bed that had multiple settings for positioning comfort. My bed had a heavy steel frame, and was set on caster wheels.

Alison found ways to escape the confinement of her crib, carefully crawling up and down the other side. It was hard to see her because of the bad lighting in the room. There was only one light fixture in the basement, and depending on which way the upstairs hallway switch was turned, sometimes you could not turn the light on to see. The switch wouldn't work half the time, so I bought a lamp.

## Locked in

One night shortly after moving in, I put Alison to sleep at the regular time, and I laid down with a book to read. The lamp went out. I put my hands out in total darkness to find the wall switch and tripped over a microphone stand that I knew had not been there seconds before. Or was I imistaken? I didn't hurt myself, but crawled over to the bathroom and tried the light there. It, too, did not work. The entire basement was pitch dark. Suddenly I became fearful. I was in a creepy basement and could not find a light to see one foot in front of my face. I heard something moving down the fifteen-foot passageway that was my closet. Shuffling sounds came from the boxes there that I had yet to unpack. Was it the kitten Karlee had found?

I made my way carefully to the stairs and walked up to the upstairs door and tried to turn the knob. It was *locked*. I did not have a key. Alison and I were locked in the basement! Was one of my sons playing a prank? I heard a new sound. Something was now under the stairs. The noise was barely audible but I could hear something moving underneath me. My heartbeat thudded in my chest. I stood there in the total darkness for a few minutes and my uneasiness grew to alarm. I felt along the wall back down to a dresser drawer, looking for a cigarette lighter. I found it! I flicked it on and saw to my astonishment that Alison's crib was now in the middle of the room! I felt the hairs on my neck tingling. How did I not hear it move? Nothing was making any sense. I looked into her bed and *she was not there!*

Now I was panicking. I rushed over to the area under the stairs and held the lighter up next to the sheathing. There was an area wide enough for her to crawl between the boards. "Peek-a-boo," Alison suddenly said in a giggly manner. I burned my hand on the hot lighter and it fell to the floor. I reached through the boards and grabbed Alison, raising my voice in disapproval, and causing her to cry. Pain, fear, and anger were becoming one.

I let out a scream for my boys that was so loud the neighbors down the street probably heard it. This only caused Alison to join me in what had to have sounded like madness in the cave-like basement—both of us screaming at the tops of our lungs. I heard Justin hurtle down the stairs. (I could recognize who walked on the stairs by the rhythm of their gait.) He opened the door—it was not locked! How was that possible? I had pulled and yanked on the door, and it had been *locked*.

The glare from upstairs shone down like a spotlight into a black cavern. I ran up the basement stairs with tears in my eyes. Justin grabbed a still screaming Alison, consoling her. I walked out the back door and out into the night, breathing heavy and clueless about the horrors that were just beginning in this house.

## The secret spirit board

I no longer conducted spirit board sessions, but episodes like that wild night were following me still. My son Jacob had the bedroom on the east wing upstairs and assisted me in some of my research. After seeing how shaken I had become after the basement incident, he told me that he was thinking of moving back to Tulsa. We had only been living in the house for a week at that point, and already he wanted out. His girlfriend Karlee was missing her mom back in Mannford, Oklahoma, and they both were not acting themselves. I attributed their behavior to being homesick. I was mistaken as to the reason why.

One Saturday afternoon I was doing research on Zozo on my laptop in the basement when I heard Jacob scream for me from upstairs. I ran upstairs as quickly as I could, wondering what in the hell could be happening *now*? Upon entering his room, I saw Karlee sobbing violently on the couch. Jacob was saying, "I'm sorry Dad, I'm sorry. I won't do it again!"

"What do you mean you won't do it again, son?" I said. "What did you do to Karlee?"

"We played with a *Ouija*, Dad," Jacob confessed. "I'm sorry. What do we do?"

"About *what*?" I asked vehemently.

I looked down at Karlee. She was rubbing her eyes and looking upward in a terrifying gaze. "I'm *blind!*" she cried. The bitter taste of fear was shared by all three of us.

I fought back my emotions and offered a calmer disposition to try and ease her unrest. "Karlee, I want you to just lie down and take some deep breaths," I said.

She did so and I looked into her eyes. They appeared glossy but otherwise normal. "It's fucking Zozo!" she exclaimed. "It said it was going to curse us all." The tears flowed from her face in long streams.

I told her to keep her eyes closed. Jacob and I sat on either side of her, holding her trembling hands.

"The sore on the cat—it said it did that, too!" Jacob said with a frightened expression.

Days before we had noticed a large ulceration on the cat's back. The kitty was already behaving like a tightly strung banshee, hissing and darting around all corners and crevices of the upstairs. The cat disappeared without a trace not long afterwards.

*It's happening again*, I realized. This home was harboring the same evil that had followed me years before. The madness was continuing! Jacob had heard of my board encounters through the years, but I kept my experiences mostly to myself. His mother and I had divorced when he was little. Now his curiosity about what had bedeviled me had led to this.

Karlee slowly regained her vision after about ten minutes of experiencing sheer terror. They showed me a homemade spirit board made from a piece of cardboard. They had been playing behind my back! Jacob regretfully confessed they were playing on the board moments before Karlee's sudden affliction—but even more troubling was their admission that they were messing with it the *night I was locked in the basement.*

I cut the board up into several pieces and threw it outside in the trash.

Jacob and Karlee moved back to Tulsa within days after the menacing Zozo told them of its curse.

A short time after they left the Oklahoma City house, Karlee and Jacob were involved in a head-on collision that very nearly ended their time on earth. On an old road outside of Mannford, Oklahoma, a careless driver crossed the center meridian and struck their small Toyota Sentra, sending both to the emergency room with life-threatening injuries.

Karlee's pelvis was broken and both of her legs were smashed. Her right arm sustained multiple open fractures. Jacob's injuries were not as severe, but left him with head trauma in more ways than one. It has taken years of recovery. I love them both very much, and I hope they can forgive me if I in some unknowing way caused some type of diabolical curse by my involvement with the dreaded Zozo.

## The Jesus painting

I went to my pastor, Kyle Peterson, who had helped me during the tragic iron tongue ordeal with my daughter, Kirsten. He gave me holy water and oil, and laid hands on me at his church. Brother Peterson and I had met by mistake, or so I thought. I was invited to a church near his and got lost, so I pulled up to his building and saw him standing outside. His eyes were penetrating. I walked up to him and asked if he knew of the church that I was seeking. He said, "I know where *my* church is, young man, why don't you join us for service?" I did.

Peterson's faith and commitment to deliverance and praise has always been a beacon of hope in a troubled world. I wish to thank him from the bottom of my heart for everything he has done for me.

I performed a deep cleansing ritual at the house that Sunday. I opened all the doors and windows, and burned wild cedar tips, sage, and sweet-grass throughout the entire place. I recited the Lord's Prayer and felt the presence of darkness flee from the house. I remember staring at the ceiling in the basement of the haunted house, both proud and fearful of what I envisioned was to come. Alison was still sneaking out of her crib and wandering the house at night while I was asleep. I am not the type of person who remembers my dreams on a nightly basis, but nightmares of losing her were happening with frequency. It became difficult to get a good night's rest. I had hung a large picture of Jesus on the wall between our beds, and it was a reminder to me of the struggle that existed between good and evil, not just in the world, but in this house and in my mind.

A month or two went by without further activity in the house. I pursued research on Zozo.

Severe storms are a common occurrence in this "tornado alley" section of Oklahoma where we were living. One night, we were hit by a violent thunderstorm. I was wakened by thunder and lightning. Oddly, Alison was in a deep sleep, not fazed by the noise. The two rectangular basement window curtains were waving angrily in the high winds. Brilliant flashes of lightning lit up the room in microsecond bursts that made my surroundings look like something in a twisted horror movie. I closed my eyes and tried to block out the nasty storm. They were soon snapped open by a sudden sound I had never heard before.

*Wooosh.... wooosh... wooosh... wooosh...*

In the darkness, I could not see the wall. Another bolt of lightning showed me an unbelievable scene. My painting of Jesus was upside down and was swaying back and forth, held by one nail. The painting was old and heavy. I had found it at a thrift store for twenty dollars weeks before. Why was it not stopping? The sound of it slashing back and forth, combined with the storm, set my adrenalin on fight or flight mode. Alison woke up with an ear-piercing scream. I jumped up, and Alison flung her little body up with arms wide open for Daddy.

I scooped her up and stood there for a few seconds, hearing the Jesus painting sway back and forth. The movement resembled the "rainbow effect" on a spirit board board, when it arcs deliberately from Z to O, Z to O. I reached out with my left arm and forced the painting to stop, my heart pounding away like a Voodoo drum.

I soon noticed the nails holding the Jesus painting were never dislodged. How it got upside down is a mystery. I would never again sleep in that basement. Alison and I moved up a level and made our room in the living area. At least there was a front door for escape!

## The snatching of Alison

Two baby gates and a door separated Alison from the basement. The ground floor became her stomping grounds. She would play with her toys and loved her little tykes table and chair I bought her. I gave her lots of crayons and color books to draw in. Her mommy and I were having problems, and I became part mom and part dad. Uncle Tom would watch her during days when I couldn't find a babysitter. Tom was about sixty-six years old and loved little Ally with a passion.

Tom fell ill in the following weeks and was in and out of the Veterans Hospital with a liver condition. In the closet of his room at the house, he found strange scratching on the walls. He called me up to view them shortly after moving in. HELP ME and KILL MOM were etched into the surface, still visible beneath the fresh paint. Who did that and why? I wondered. There were no answers. The wallpaper was a striped pattern that indicated that a child had once lived in his room. Tom complained of nightmares, and his electronics acting strangely.

We had to call an ambulance several times because Tom's condition became severe. Watching the paramedics carry him down those narrow stairs was quite an eerie site. A standard gurney would not work on the stairs. They had to wrap him up in several sheets and carefully swing him down like a living mummy. We all wondered how much longer Tom had.

At one point, on Tom's advice, I called the landlord and asked if there was anything they would like to tell me about this place. Asked what I meant, I explained why we thought the place was haunted. A long uncomfortable pause ensued. The landlord reluctantly informed me that they had purchased the home from a couple with mental issues. She went on to explain that the troubled home owners had several children who also suffered ailments. The younger children had advanced mental retardation. As I mentioned earlier, these people had departed abruptly in the middle of the night, never to be heard from again. The fact that they had left so many personal belongings left me wondering if they also had experienced something evil in this creaky old house.

Tom's condition finally resulted in full blown cancer. It got so bad I would have to carry him to the bathroom. Many nights I was awakened by Tom bellowing out in immense pain. I had never seen a person's health deteriorate so quickly. Watching my dear Uncle Tom die was one of the hardest things I have ever had to endure. The house became a rest home of horrors. One evening, another ambulance arrived to take Tom to the hospital, where he collapsed and was pronounced dead. I loved Uncle Tom and his death haunts me to this day.

One afternoon, I was upstairs talking to Justin. I kept peeking around the corner downstairs at Alison, who was playing hide and seek. I was telling my son of a house we were contracted to work on, when I heard Ally scream bloody murder. I hurled my body towards the stairway and saw her *lifted up by unseen hands and whisked away violently*. I raced down the stairs and turned the corner. I could only hear her screams leading towards the basement! I barreled through the kitchen towards the next corner, and then froze. Alison was only a scream, still not visible. I prayed out loud, begging God to shield her from harm. I could hear Alison underneath the stairs like she was in severe pain.

This time, I could not reach her through the boards. It was if she were pinned to the cellar wall. I frantically beat the shit out of the boards until they broke in. I pulled her out, still screaming and now kicking. I began to cry. Praying and sobbing, I took her back upstairs into Tom's room. Justin was close behind with a baseball bat, fearful that some unseen assailant was trying to kidnap his baby sister. Within an hour, Justin boarded up the door leading to the basement.

Later, we put our money together and took our belongings from the basement that would fit on the stairs and moved them to the top floor. I got Alison to sleep by reading her a story from one of Tom's books. I put her down and placed the book back onto Tom's shelf. I noticed a notebook and opened it up. On the front page I saw in Tom's handwriting, "Tell Alison I love her." It was like a ghost had written this message from beyond. I cried myself to sleep that night.

The chilling events that occurred in that house left a profound effect on me that I can still feel years later. As I write this, tears are flowing. I regret moving my loved ones into that place. Nothing but craziness and bad luck happened to all of us while living there.

## Update on the haunted house

In 2016, I made contact with a woman named Tricia, who said she and her family had owned and lived at the haunted house before me for eighteen years. She and her family experienced haunting phenomena, but said they attributed it to a man they believed was buried beneath the front porch.

"He's there looking for his wife and daughter," Tricia told me. "We lived there from 1987 to 2005. A little after we moved in—I was fourteen at the time—there was an old speaker at the top of the stairs going up to the top floor. At night we would hear it making a beeping noise. And then we would hear people talking on it. So my father got up there and saw that it was just there and not hooked to any wires or anything. So he took it out.

"Then about a week later, I was standing in the kitchen doing the dishes and I saw a man walk in the back door. I looked at him and I could see the wall behind him. I was in shock so I just stood there. It felt like an hour later he finally walked down the back stairs to the basement. He was wearing blue jeans flannel shirt and a cowboy hat. I ran to my mother up on the top floor. We both searched the garage and the basement, and he wasn't there."

"How did you find out about the body buried there?" I asked.

"Me and mom were digging next to the porch to plant some flowers," Tricia said. We dug down a couple of feet and she hit something hard and concrete. So we dug it up and cleaned it up. It was an old, old headstone. We saw his name. The dates we couldn't see. So we went to the courthouse downtown and did some research, and found out that the house was sitting on a family plot."

"So there could be more bodies buried on that plot?"

"Yes," Tricia said. "We only found that one headstone. We had planned on breaking up the concrete out front to see if we could find any more, but we never got around to it."

I asked Tricia about the scratched messages we had found in the upstairs closet in the room that had been Uncle Tom's bedroom.

"They were already there when we moved in," she answered. "They were in my bedroom closet."

"Do you remember what those scratchings said?" I asked.

She said, "I hate Mama, and Help. There were others, but those are the ones I remember. My father wanted to remove the old, old, old wallpaper where some of those scratchings were in my room."

I asked Tricia if she or any members of her family had ever used a spirit board while living in the house. She said they had not.

"What other strange stuff can you remember?"

"The stairway was where we heard the most sounds," Tricia said. "It was every day and night. The sound of cowboy boots constantly running up and down the stairs. It drove us crazy.

"We would always find odd things in and around the house. Odd jars and glasses, old coins that weren't there days earlier. We would find old newspaper clippings. We had no idea where they came from. We mostly found stuff in the crawl space in the basement."

"That's where my little girl would crawl and hide!" I exclaimed.

"My parents did not like that crawl space," Tricia said. "They forbid my brothers and I from going there after we kept finding stuff."

She went on, "I had a dream about the ghost I saw, which I believe to be the guy buried out front. He told me that he wasn't there to harm anybody. He's in the house looking for his wife and daughter. His daughter's name was the same as mine, and she looked a lot like me."

"Did the floors make noises?"

"Oh my God, yes, I hated those floors! They squeaked like crazy all the time. And the sound of cowboy boots walking everywhere. The basement was Mom and Dad's room. They would hear things down there all the time."

"Did you ever experience anything with pictures or wall hangings?"

"Yes! they never stayed on the walls or they would go sideways. I have OCD [obsessive compulsive disorder], so I was always having to fix them. We also found out downtown [at the courthouse] that the house was converted from an old hospital. We never found out what kind, though."

After speaking at length with Tricia, I called the county assessor's office. Their files on the house only verify that it was built in 1940. They show no notes on anything. I was unable to verify any burial plot or conversion from a hospital.

Tricia gave me the name on the headstone, which, pending verification, I will keep confidential.

Even if the story about the headstone and old burial plot cannot be validated, it is still significant that occupants of the house prior to me and my family experienced haunting phenomena. There was definitely something going on inside that house.

# 5

## Pursuing Zozo Around the World

My experiences with Zozo compelled me to find out if there were others like me. I refused to believe that I was alone.

In 2008, while living in Ft. Smith, Arkansas, I started a blog on some of my experiences and research into the Zozo Phenomenon. I told others about my many malevolent experiences with a spirit board entity that called itself Zozo, and how these experiences had taken me down a very dark road and made me wonder about my own sanity. I realized that it all sounded more like something from the twisted mind of a horror novelist, rather than something that could happen in real life—and to anyone.

In the beginning, I was jokingly referred to as a "Zozologist." Many people did not take me seriously. In those early days, I would post my experiences in paranormal chat rooms and on message boards, and sometimes I would be laughed off the internet due to the sheer perceived craziness of what I was revealing. When word spread that I intended to write this book, skeptics responded that perhaps a better usage of the paper would be to wad it up and cram it down my throat. Reading those words, I remember feeling the sting of personal attack, but smiled knowing my findings would speak for themselves.

I kept going, no matter what others thought and said. Like an old bird dog, I sniffed around, catching the scent of something sinister in the air. I dug up old bones and added new ones to my collection along the hunt, covering long stretches of territory. I scoured the internet.

I discovered that Zozo was mentioned as an actual demon in a nineteenth-century book of French demonology called *The Dictionnaire Infernal*, written in various editions. For the first time in my research, I had come across something historic. The details surrounding this important discovery are chronicled later in this book.

And finally, I found another Zozo encounter. *I was not alone in my nightmare.* I felt a profound sense of relief.

I dug deeper. I found more references to an entity that referred to itself as Zozo, coming through spirit board sessions. I found this both disturbing and fascinating, because I realized I definitely was not alone!

I knew beyond a shadow of a doubt that these accounts were beyond coincidence, and I continued my search for answers. Soon I was collecting stories from other countries, all telling of run-ins with this dark character, Zozo.

What was Zozo? I still did not know for certain. Was it a demon, as it had told me? In my communications with it, Zozo referred to itself as a "king of kings," a ruler of paradise. In many of my sessions, Zozo said that it wanted to take us to this paradise. When we asked where was paradise, it always spelled the same answer: HELL.

In my blog, I encouraged people to send me their Zozo stories to share, and received more emails than I could have imagined. In several of these, this paradise reference was repeated. In nearly all the stories, Zozo surfaced on a spirit board, and then strange events would take place. Bizarre run-ins with this still little-known entity streamed in from Canada, the United Kingdom, and even Australia. I posted some of them on the site. I began looking into things like linguistics, ancient religions, and the various pantheons and hierarchies of demons and evil spirits.

One pattern that surfaced was quite disturbing. Over and over again, I found that "Zozo effects" linger, sometimes for long periods after board use has stopped. I heard from many others who told me they thought Zozo was around them all the time, just waiting for another opportunity to come through the board—or anything else. I knew what they were talking about—I lived through it myself.

As for who Zozo picked on, the targets were probably the easiest persons to affect. The reasons why could be many, and they are discussed more later in this book. But I saw this pattern emerge repeatedly, too.

It also became apparent that more than casual board users were involved in the Zozo Phenomenon. Paranormal investigators contacted me after having encountered Zozo in the course of their investigations. Here is one case:

> My name is Dan Cormany and I am a paranormal investigator and part-time demonologist located in Sykesville, Maryland. I have devoted my life to investigating, studying, and researching the paranormal world and am currently operating my own paranormal investigation and research team, Knight-Time Paranormal (KTP).
>
> My team and I have had multiple encounters with this demon and would like to share them with you. My team is well-rounded and is very skilled in the field. The main members of KTP are myself, Mike Slein, and Jason Jones. We have roughly nine years of experience each and have investigated hundreds of haunted locations in the continental United States and internationally. We have also investigated alongside many well-known and reputable paranormal teams such as: North Texas Paranormal Research Society, Ghost Adventures Crew, TAPS, and Ghost Lab.
>
> Knight-Time Paranormal encountered ZOZO for the first time during an investigation of an old hotel in Indiana while conducting an Ouija board session (I am not legally allowed to give the name of the hotel or the other party involved).
>
> My partner and co-founder of Knight-Time Paranormal, Mike, tells it best:
>
> "Immediately after we began the Ouija board session, I felt something. I always feel something whenever we do a Ouija board session or a summoning ritual, but I had never felt something this strong and negative in my career. As the session progressed, I started hearing voices whispering things in my ear that

I couldn't understand. This happened continuously and finally I spoke out and asked who was talking. I had to know who it was. That was when things got weird and slightly terrifying. The person sitting directly across from me (the owner of the hotel) became very quiet and still with a blank expression on his face.

"After several moments of dead silence, he spoke and said that we had summoned something very evil (scary). At that exact moment we were all startled by a very loud and ground-shaking bang. The table shlfted dramatically, as if someone (or something) was pushing it. The Ouija board began spelling out gibberish words and random numbers (however, I did notice that 666 came through several times). The room became ice cold and I could physically feel a dark and very evil entity enter the room. I became legitimately scared when the planchette began sliding back and forth across the board landing on the letters Z-O-Z-O-Z-O-Z-O, and the image of what turned out to be ZOZO entered my mind.

"ZOZO told me that it was here and that it wasn't leaving. I asked it why it was speaking to me and no one else (which caused the others to become very fearful). ZOZO then told me that I was going to be involved in a great tragedy and that my life was to come to an end very soon. I asked it what it meant (out loud), and it said that it could help me.

"Suddenly Jason spoke (seemingly to ZOZO) and said, 'You're lying. You're deceiving us.' That made things much worse. The board became extremely hot and we had to pull our hands back. ZOZO then told me that it was going to ruin us all because we had disturbed it. Oddly, we all placed our hands back on the planchette at the same exact time and Dan asked if ZOZO would show itself. The board spelled out M-I-R-R-O-R and we were puzzled. To our knowledge, there was no mirror in the room. But then Jason looked at the far wall and noticed a mirror leaning against it. A mirror that had not been there when we arrived. We all watched in shock as an apparition of a large human-like figure manifested itself and the letter Z appeared in a strange mist the had formed on the top left corner of the mirror. The figure had a contorted and ugly face and its body was twisted and appeared to have scorched skin. I was staring at a demon that was so evil, it had almost killed someone several years ago and had caused many people to abandon their places of dwelling. I had to maintain courage and not give it the energy it wanted.

"Then the figure disappeared...along with the mirror. Not long after that, we decided enough was enough and we closed the session and tossed drops of holy water around the room. I still felt the dark energy that I felt at the start and knew that ZOZO had attached itself to me. For several weeks after that encounter, I felt that I was being followed. I would see shadows in my house at random times. I would have horrible nightmares with images of ZOZO. Finally, I sought help from a priest and had myself and my house blessed. ZOZO left me alone but I have not fully ridden myself of the attachment and I don't think I ever will."

Stories like this had a big impact on me. Not only was I not alone, but others had experienced some of the hell I had been through. Was Zozo really a demon? How many other people was it pestering? Judging from the flood of stories that were coming in—a lot. I was determined to get to the bottom of it.

After reading many stories like the one above, I had to wonder, was Zozo riding along with me, too, like an invisible ticking time bomb? I had given up the spirit board, yet the creepy phenomena were still tormenting me. On several occasions, I backed away from my research, trying to distance myself from anything associated with Zozo. I just had to give myself some breathing room. But I always got pulled back in. Zozo was a lure that I could not ignore.

After about a year of collecting encounters with Zozo, I contacted Dave Schrader of the popular *Darkness on the Edge of Town* paranormal radio show. I sent him an email about my experiences and the research I had done to date. He quickly responded and invited me to be a guest. I remember being quite nervous about being on a real radio show talking about all of this, but Dave was an experienced and insightful host and put me at ease. We talked about some of my frightening encounters, and Dave revealed that someone from his engineering department had their own puzzling Zozo experience on a spirit board! Talk about more validation!

A strange thing happened during this broadcast. I did not feel well prepared for the interview, as I had been working on a jobsite earlier that day and had left my cell phone charger on the home owners' back porch. I did not have much battery power going into the show, but amazingly it lasted for the whole hour. The split second the interview was over, the phone went dead and never worked again! Did it have any connection to the fact that I did the show in my son Justin's bedroom in the haunted Oklahoma City house? Perhaps it was just a coincidence, but an odd one, nonetheless.

Even stranger, I learned that after the show Dave contacted prominent demonologist John Zaffis to find out what he knew about Zozo. John is the nephew of Ed and Lorraine Warren, paranormal investigators who rose to international fame for the high profile demonic cases they took on. The couple was very upfront about their warnings to people in regards to using a spirit board. John learned the ropes from his famous aunt and uncle, and then struck out on his own to develop an outstanding career in the paranormal. (Ed died in 2006, and Lorraine retired in 2016. Some of their most famous cases have been turned into films.)

John came on *Darkness At the Edge of Town* radio the following week to help shed light on the Zozo Phenomenon. I listened in with nervous anticipation. I had heard of John from my research into demonology, and had come across videos of him warning people to be cautious when using boards because dangerous entities could come through.

John revealed on the show that he had indeed heard of Zozo from his years of experience investigating hauntings. He also explained that it was common to experience an odd synchronicity within related paranormal events. Here Zozo was a topic on the radio, he noted, and then he dropped a bomb in that he had recently investigated two separate Zozo cases involving females who were having issues.

This was *huge*! It immediately gave my research more validity. Here was a leading expert in demonology and the paranormal confirming that Zozo was a real phenomenon. I was stunned.

The buzz from that show motivated me to dig deeper. Zaffis and I had a few lively conversations, and even did a few more radio interviews together where people would call in and share their experiences and ask questions. Overnight I went from a paranormal laughingstock to someone doing radio interviews with respected individuals who were intrigued by my story. The buzz spread about this strange entity and the paranormal activity that would sometimes manifest when it surfaced on boards. I ramped up efforts to learn more about demonology.

## Explosion of website traffic

I also installed site tracking technology on my Zozo Phenomenon website. Obviously, the interest was growing. I kept noticing unusual page visits from all over the world. In just over a year the site had over a quarter of a million visits, and many were from prominent universities and government offices. What was going on? I would spend hours typing in the latitude and longitudinal coordinates from visitors who were spending lots of time on the site and tracing their whereabouts to some very interesting locations, including Tel Aviv, Israel; the Red Square in Moscow; desolate areas in South Africa; and other places I never even knew existed. I quickly surpassed the Google search engine ranking of a film called *Zozo*, released in 2005, about a Lebanese boy who was separated from his family during the civil war and winds up in Sweden.

During this period, I noticed that half the visits were from URLs that had been blocked or were unidentifiable. All that the tracking software would show was what search words were used in order to pull up my website. I saw that someone from Salt Lake City Utah was landing on the site for hours at a time. After a few weeks of observation, I was able to determine that this person logged on and off at the exact same times as myself. How strange!

I tracked the visits to St. Ann's Catholic Church. I would log onto my site for three minutes, then off for three minutes, and check the site tracker. The log-ins would be identical each time I checked! Then it dawned on me—that someone was *me*!

I had heard of mirrored domain names, but how could someone be mirroring my computer connection's URL and making it look like I was logging on eight hundred miles away? This was an unnerving thought. I looked up the number to the church and called it. No answer. The next day my logins registered back to Oklahoma City, where I lived. Hmmm, a Catholic Church? It just did not make sense.

Weird experiences like this happen all the time to people who become involved in the paranormal. It's as though some colossal Trickster plays game with you. And, as I had discovered and would continue to see play out over the years, Zozo has quite a trickster nature.

There was more. I also noted visits from various Vatican offices in Italy, including the American advisor to the Pope! Everything was getting crazy, and the page visits were rising, averaging five hundred visits per day from all corners of the Earth. The interest in Zozo was incredible, and I felt a responsibility to post more professional research, so I put on my detective hat again.

What I found led me down a twisting, bizarre path of strange connections: the quirks of the letter Z, the power in names, and the associations between Zozo and magic, Aleister Crowley, and Jimmy Page. I discovered that Zozo has many alter egos, and that the word "zozo" has dark associations throughout history, and around the world. The deeper I went, the more complex became the mystery of Zozo. Soon, I learned, there would be no easy answers. Zozo hides behind many masks.

I submitted an article describing some of my early experiences to a popular ghost stories website, and it caught the attention of a group of film makers in Los Angeles. They contacted me by email asking if I would be interested in discussions pertaining to a horror script based on the various Zozo encounters I had documented on my site. My research was being noticed by a lot of people!

The Zozo stories continued to surface, and the California film company persisted.

# 6

## Zozo the Movie Star

Soon I reached a point where I had to back away again, and so put my Zozo research on hold. About eight months went by with nothing that I would attribute to paranormal activity happening to me or any of my friends or family. I kept in contact with the writer and producer who wanted to do a film based on the Zozo Phenomenon. They wanted to cast me in the movie portraying myself, a paranormal researcher/survivor. Zack Coffman and Scott Di'Lalla were both involved as independent film makers, specializing in documentaries that catered to motorcycle enthusiasts. They were confident and passionate about their work, and that enthusiasm was contagious. I agreed to appear in a small but significant role. We all felt it would be cool to portray myself as someone trying to help a fearful victim of a Zozo board encounter.

It was not money that motivated me to appear in the film, as none was offered. I had asked for ten thousand dollars because of all the awareness and hype that I generated on the internet. My site was getting a lot of web traffic, and I had managed to push my internet presence on Google search engines to the number one spot on the front page of anything associated with the keyword "Zozo." That sum simply was not within the budget of the film, and they explained that they were literally selling DVDs of some of their documentaries from the trunks of their vehicles at biker events. I was at a crossroads. I liked both of these men, but felt my involvement was worth more than a free performance. I threatened to distance myself from the project.

Zack and Scott told me they would move on with the film with or without me, so after much consideration, I made the decision to become involved. Looking back, I think I made the right decision.

For the filming, I had to go to One World Studios in Seattle. I arrived at the airport in November 2010 during a snowstorm. Zack and Scott were both outstanding hosts and a lot of fun to hang out with. The whole time I was looking for signs that it was the right thing to do. The first night, I was talking with the ever enthusiastic Scott (cameraman, director, and writer), and the light in the room began to flicker. Scott gave me a surprised look and I told him that kind of thing could be expected when dealing with Zozo.

We went for walks through the buzzing metropolis of Seattle. For a struggling, long-haired hippie from Oklahoma, I felt like I was part of something larger than myself.

## George and the vanishing raven

My scene was to be filmed at what was once a huge Masonic retirement center located on Marine View Drive in Des Moines, Washington, along the banks of Puget Sound. The building was colossal, constructed of copper and slate, terra cotta, and marble. The interior featured box beam ceilings, hand-carved woodworking, and elegant stained glass. It had been built in 1926 The hallways were long and extraordinary. The place reminded me of scenes where Jack Nicholson stalked his family in the horror classic film, *The Shining*.

No one lived there anymore. The new owners used the building as an event center for weddings and other occasions. Only twenty-five percent of it was functional and the rest was vacant. Or so we were told.

The south wing of the third floor was where my part was filmed. The historic building was filled with vacant apartments, none of which had their own bathrooms. Each residential floor had a large communal bathroom.

There were entire sections of the place that were roped off with signs that said RESTRICTED AREA DO NOT PASS. I thought the whole place was a nine on a creepy scale of ten.

I was nervous about the rehearsals, so while I waited for my turn, I wandered around the building in spite of the warning signs. What could it hurt?

I went down to the musty basement. Rows and rows of vintage medical equipment and boxes with warning labels littered the labyrinthine passageways down there. I wondered if I would get lost. I heard faint voices. There were strange, sharp smells. I was getting more and more creeped out by the experience when I was interrupted by a disheveled looking elderly woman. "You don't belong down here," she grunted. There was something menacing by the gleaming look in her eyes and her thin-lipped expression. Her hair resembled Albert Einstein's, but matted as well as frizzy. I didn't say a word, but did an abrupt about face and briskly trotted my way back down the corridors and back up to the palatial ground floor.

No more exploring! I hopped in the elevator and pressed the number three. It was almost my time to be filmed, and I had to pee. The elevator door opened and I came out, expecting to see a crew member, a sound guy, *someone*. Wait…this was not the third floor. It was the second. It was deserted. I had to go! I walked down the hall and found the bathroom. Inside was a row of about five stalls, each with hospital curtains on swivel rollers separating the toilets. I walked to the end of the bathroom and saw a final curtain. I slid it back and saw a urinal. Yay! I was relieving myself when out of the blue the curtain was *yanked violently* behind me. In mid-stream, I almost buckled over from the surprise.

There was *no one there!* I was reaching down to zip up when it hit me. What I can only describe as an organ cramp brought me to my knees. The pain was excruciating and felt like a horse kick. I yelled out for help. The pain got worse. I started to pray aloud, like I had done before during times of extreme fear, but the words would not come. I forced myself, questioning my sanity. "G, G, George help me," I stuttered! George? What the hell? I was trying to say Jesus, but it just wouldn't come. "J, J, J Jorge help me! Again this name was pronounced.... was I losing my mind?

As quickly as it came, the cramp subsided and I gasped. I staggered out of the bathroom from hell with my zipper undone and piss dribbling down my jeans. I held up my pants as I pressed the elevator button. I had to get out of this place!

After what seemed like an eternity, the elevator opened. I must have pressed the star for level one a hundred times before the door opened again. What nightmarish world would I walk into next? I desperately needed some fresh air and a cigarette. I could see the huge front double doors and I scrambled outside like I was escaping a mental institution during a fire drill.

I walked. I breathed. I lit a cigarette. I heard an animated laughter that sounded like Burgess Meredith as The Joker in the old Batman series. "Wah wah wah" again and again.

I gazed towards the sky and beheld a large raven perched in a small tree. His head was bobbing up and down with each chuckle, as if he knew what had just taken place. I thought of "George" again. Why did I say this name?

Suddenly the grounds were literally alive with murders of ravens. In Oklahoma we have crows, but not these ravens with their amazing intellect and magical auras. The one perched in the tree was still looking at me, laughing away. I slowly walked towards the tree and took out my cell phone. I wanted to capture this raucous noise and behavior. I pressed record and stood there filming. The bird quit laughing and took its eyes off of me and looked away. It dove downward and then the most amazing thing happened right before the camera's eye. *It vanished into thin air!*

Everything around me felt weird, as though I had gone into another dimension. I was a stranger in a strange land. *What kind of place was this?* I was stricken by what had just happened in less than thirty minutes. Was I hallucinating again? I walked around the gardens and sat down on a bench to look at my video of the raven. I played it several times looking for a flight path, or to see if it disappeared behind something, but the raven simply disappeared. I uploaded this video to You Tube and it caught the attention of producers of the popular paranormal show *Fact or Faked*, and they featured it on an episode. They examined the footage and could not make any claims of it being faked. The footage was never altered or tampered with in any way. It remains on YouTube, and you can watch it by searching for the keywords *Zozo Raven*.

Did I capture something supernatural? I have since received a few emails from people claiming to have witnessed similar events with ravens. Did I become the laughingstock of a shapeshifting demon bird? It was like it *knew* I had been on the receiving end of some kind of spiritual attack inside this building. I thought of the mysterious jars that I found encircling the original Zozo witch board. Did the raven jump into another dimension? Could this be the spirit of one of those birds found preserved next to the dreaded double-sided Ouija?

I went back into the spooky building and stopped in the office to talk to the day manager. I told her I had wandered down into the basement and saw a very strange-looking old woman. She gave me a scolding look and said it was against the rules for any visitors to go into the basement or any other restricted areas. She said there was no one allowed down there, *including faculty members!* I apologized.

She offered me a look of concern. "You seem a bit pale, are you feeling well?" she asked.

I said I had had a weird experience in one of the bathrooms. She paused for a moment and I sensed an uncomfortable silence. I explained to her that I was a paranormal researcher and that the film we were shooting was based on my experiences and research.

She told me there was only one ghost hunting team that she was aware of that had ever investigated the location. "Something scared the team members so much they left abruptly in the middle of the night," she said.

"What happened?"

"Well, we really don't know, but there are rooms in this place that even the housekeepers and maintenance people refuse to go into. The basement is one such area. Have you been on the third floor?"

"Not yet," I said." I am about to head that way to film my scenes."

"Oh, you will be in room 307," she answered. "It is one of the rooms people are afraid of. It is haunted by George."

I was stunned. I could offer no words, and I did not even try. The chills crept over me like a hundred roaches on my skin, and I felt a wave of nausea flow over me.

This time I took the stairs all the way to the third floor and found room 307. I saw some writing just below the numbers. Someone had written the name *George* on the door. I finished my scenes for *I Am Zozo* and then assisted the director by carrying gear back down to the lobby. I found a more modern public restroom on the ground floor, and washed my hands. There was a window on the far side overlooking the back grounds. Something told me to go look outside.

I knew there was something else I needed to see. I approached the window and looked through.

Outside was an old man, hunched over walking with a cane. His head was down and he appeared to be disabled. I just stood there watching him when suddenly he looked straight up towards me with the most sinister expression I have ever seen. I snapped backward out of view, then decided to peek one more time outside. The window gave a full panoramic view of the grounds that covered two acres of the property.

The old man was gone.

I never found out who the crazy-looking old woman was. I asked the faculty member in the main office on the ground floor if anyone was down there and she made a call. The one housekeeper on duty said she had not been down in the basement.

## A film fizzle

The post production of the film dragged on for a long time, and then finally it was released worldwide on DVD. For the overseas markets, the title was changed to *Are You There?* I'm not sure why. Despite the hype generated on the internet, the film did not live up to the excitement. It received bad ratings.

When I had first read the script, I thought it was well-written and seemed creepy enough, but I felt the creep factor never really played out on screen. We had filmed some scenes that I wished had made the final cut, because I thought they were scarier than the ones that were chosen. The film was also shot on Kodak's new 8-mm film, which gave it a spooky "old school look." *I Am Zozo* was the first feature length film to do so, and I think it did add to the ambience of the film.

The events that happened on location of *I Am Zozo* are more frightening to me than the movie itself. I would like to thank the guys at One World Studios for inviting me to be a part of their film.

# 7

## Television Adventures

The Zozo film may not have made a big splash, but a bigger media exposure soon came along, and generated a flood of controversy. When the producers of *Ghost Adventures* approached me in 2014 about doing an episode, I never intended to get back on a spirit board as part of the show. I was okay with joining Zak Bagans and the cast and crew for an investigation, but the thought of actually using a board struck me as courting disaster. Nearly a decade had passed since I had last touched one. My wife, Kathleen (we were still together), was equally apprehensive about doing the show.

The episode was going to be filmed in Oklahoma City at the haunted house where I had had so many of my nightmarish experiences. We hadn't lived there in years, and merely revisiting the house was freaky enough. I decided to do the show as a way of warning others about Zozo and the dangerous spirits that can be contacted on spirit boards.

I took Kathleen with me to meet the crew in the backyard of the house. Kathleen had made no plans to be a part of the show, but agreed to come along for support. We were told that Zak Bagans,

Aaron Goodwin, and Nick Groff would be coming to meet us and do preliminary interviews. When I saw Zak, I was a little nervous. He came walking up quickly with lighted cameras behind him. He was intense, all business. His eyes beamed with curiosity.

Zak seemed to carry a presence with him. He had a big energy field and persona. I don't know if it was due to all the investigations he has conducted, or if it is just his personality. They were all very cool to hang out with, and I did not know what to expect with Zak, but he was very cordial to Kathleen and myself.

I had never agreed in advance to get back on a Ouija for this investigation, but Zak pressed the issue with cameras rolling. I thought about it for a few moments and then agreed to take the risk. Kathleen did not like my decision. She was asked to join us on camera for the lock-down part of the show, and I was not too happy about that. So, we were both on edge as the filming began.

Kathleen has always been vulnerable to sudden changes in behavior brought on by anxiety and stress. I take responsibility for the decision to include her in this investigation, but in reflection I think it was a bad error in judgment on my part. Kathleen was overcome with emotion. She also had been sick before making the trip from Tulsa to Oklahoma City. Her coughing is evident in the episode. Clearly, she should not have been a part of the investigation, something that became increasingly evident as the night wore on.

Strange thumps greeted us before we even walked through the front door. The house was empty, so what could be making any noise? The weird sounds did not let up, but continued well into the night. The fear in that place was heavy and contagious. There were no scripts, no rehearsals. The events that were filmed that night were unsettling.

Our Ouija board had been loaned to us for the show by Robert Murch, one of the world's leading experts on the Ouija and its history. When Nick Groff and I sat down to use it, we both looked at each other like we were crazy. Robert had said the board was sent to him by a man who claimed to have been repeatedly raped by a demonic force after making board contact with Zozo. *Thanks, Murch*, I thought wryly.

I had met with Murch the day before filming at the hotel where we were staying. Robert was in town to be interviewed for the episode. Here I was, about to be on the most popular paranormal television program in the world, and I was shaking hands with the world's foremost expert on Ouija boards. We had had several amazing conversations over the years but had never met, and now meeting him face to face was just so cool! He showed me a small part of his huge Ouija collection, and handed me what he called the "pre-Ouija," a rare prototype board that he said was only one of two known in existence. I had interviewed Murch on my paranormal radio show and found him to be very witty and an incredible source of information on everything Ouija.

For the Ouija session, we went upstairs to the bedroom I had always called the "safe room," where I used to retreat whenever phenomena in the house got overwhelming. We put the Ouija and planchette on the floor. Nick and I would work the board. We had cameras on us the entire time. Also, downstairs, crew members were monitoring cameras and recorders that had been set up throughout the house.

None of us knew what was going to happen. Nick and I placed our hands on the planchette. Another unexplained thud sounded outside the room. Nick commented that he felt like some kind of electric static energy was running through his body. Sitting in a darkened room with the *Ghost Adventures* cast in the freaking house where I had had so many bad experiences was *insane!*

Several minutes went by before we got a response on the planchette. Meanwhile, there were sounds of footsteps on the stairs. Kathleen became agitated and showed signs of anxiety. Nick commented that he felt as though something had gone through his body.

The planchette began to move on its own. Nick looked at me like he was in another world. We asked if there was something with us, and the planchette slowly moved to YES. I was hoping it was not my old nemesis. I asked for its name. The planchette moved with greater intensity towards the left—I was sitting with the board upside down to me—and I closed my eyes until it stopped on the letter Z. It then scooted right, and I knew what was there. Everyone felt it. The centerpiece began to move in what I coined "the rainbow effect" from Z to O, back and forth, back and forth. Zozo was back!

Nick and I were not moving the planchette purposefully. He said repeatedly that he could tell neither of us was deliberately guiding the triangular device. It was evident to us that we were not controlling the movements—some other force that was in that room was doing so. Another loud thud sounded.

Kathleen was not in any shape to be in that house with me using a Ouija, and after a short while, she could not take it any longer. She got up and left, saying she needed some air. We heard her go down the stairs and out the front door. Cameras captured her saying, "Fuck this house!"

We continued the session. We all felt body chills. The strange noises in the house continued. At one point, one of the legs fell off the planchette.

We heard Kathleen return and come up the stairs. Nick commented that he felt something was not right about her. When she appeared in the room, she seemed to be a different person. You could hear it in her voice. She interrupted the session. I noticed her belt was undone, and she was barefoot. She did not seem to be aware of either until it was pointed out to her.

A foul smell like rotting flesh and sulfur followed her entrance. I read some negative comments on social media after the episode aired on The Travel Channel, in which people thought Kathleen had shit outside, but I know better. Kathleen *never* put off a foul smell. And this odor was not one of shit. I had never smelled anything like it, and everyone present noticed it as well.

Kathleen said Zozo had told her to come back upstairs. She shocked us by revealing that she had been sexually assaulted outside, apparently by Zozo, who was "very sexual." She sat for a few minutes in discomfort, and then got up and left again, hurrying down the stairs and outside.

I know it came across that I was unconcerned about her, but that was not the case. After about ten minutes, I told the crew I needed to go check on her. Zak and I went outside, but she was nowhere in sight.

Alarmed, we jumped into a vehicle and drove up and down the streets for half an hour searching for Kathleen. Finally, she called me on my cell phone and told me she was back at the hotel. She was safe.

We returned to the house and went back upstairs to do another session on the board. One of the crew, Jay Wasley, had had a bad board experience and wanted to work the board with me to find out more information. In response to a question, the entity—presumably Zozo—said that its intent toward Jay was KILL.

The bangs, thumps, and rattling sounds continued while we worked the board. At one point, Zozo laughed HA HA, and also spelled out NICK G. GOODBYE. Ironically, this would be the last episode for the long-standing *Ghost Adventures* investigator. Did Zozo know this would be his final investigation with the team? The planchette whirled in circles. We all decided we needed to get fresh air, and closed the session. We were all exhausted from that house—it had a way of draining you physically and mentally.

When the show aired in 2015 (Episode 3 of Season 10), more was featured, including the interview with Murch and a brief experiment with a handy man who did not like house.

Hundreds of people reported experiencing strange events while watching "The Zozo Demon" episode, including paranormal phenomena, bizarre behavior in pets that were present during the show, and a myriad of creepy occurrences. The episode was reportedly the scariest episode in the ten-season history of the series. Ratings went through the roof.

Thousands of comments were shared on social media. Never in internet history had a demonic name ever trended on social media, but this was exactly what happened during the show. The Zozo Demon episode allegedly caused people to vomit, and many others reported that they felt ill watching the show. Some said could not watch the entire episode. Hundreds of people commented they felt very disturbed while watching it, and then had nightmares.

It cannot be determined how many of these reactions might have been subconsciously self-induced, however. If people are primed to believe that they will be adversely affected simply by watching a television show, they may fulfill their own expectations. Nonetheless, it was clear to me that Zozo had the capability of reaching out beyond the screen.

I received an avalanche of emails from people, like the following story from a woman:

> Back in the mid-nineties I bought a Ouija board to use by myself. When I began using it, the planchette would move randomly around the board not spelling words. Like gibberish. After several days of random letters, the planchette began using vowels.
>
> Until I saw your episode of *Ghost Adventures* I thought nothing of it spelling ZOZOZO. I thought it may not be English. It was very uneventful other than that. I am glad I did not know what it meant then.
>
> During the next few weeks, subtle things happened. My rain stick made the full raining sound while

it was propped against the fireplace. I heard three distinct knocks on my closet door in the middle of the night. An ice cold feeling woke me up once.

Then, several weeks later, my three-year-old son, Mark, started having nightmares. He wanted to sleep in bed between my then husband and me.

Once, in the middle of the night, Mark and I awoke at the same time. It turned out we were having the same nightmare about a black snake.

The incident that came next scared me so badly. About 4 AM, Mark sat straight up in bed and said, "Mommy, will you die for us?"

I was afraid to move. And next day extreme guilt came over me. Mark was asleep right after he said it, so he didn't remember a thing.

Who the hell is "us" and why should I die? I just can't figure out why my baby would say this. I know it was not Mark.

Whether this type of phenomena is something that goes hand in hand with Zozo, I don't know. Thank you for letting me get this off my chest.

Zozo often talks about killing, dying, and taking over a person, and it is capable of invading dreams. It is not possible to know how many people who watched the show got the shock of their lives when they became part of the Zozo Phenomenon.

## Aftershocks

Bagans and I talked about the episode on his follow-up series, *Ghost Adventures: Aftershocks*. We both agreed that it was quite unnerving that Zozo became an occult part of history by being the first demonic name to ever trend on Twitter. Zak wrote in his book, *I Am Haunted*, that he suspects I have an attachment to Zozo but I am unaware of it. He doesn't know me very well.

I have no doubt that whole experience deeply troubled Kathleen. A month after filming for *Ghost Adventures*, Kathleen had several episodes of violent behavior that landed her in a great deal of difficulty. I revealed her troubles on *Aftershocks*.

As I write these words, I cannot help but wonder if my involvement in the Zozo Phenomenon cursed Kathleen and other family members. It was never my intention for anyone to get hurt. Two of my best friends have died in exactly the manner the entity had prophesied, and now I have in effect lost my second wife.

## Aftershocks with Jamie

After the *Ghost Adventures* episode, I had an opportunity to talk to my first wife, Jamie, in person about it. Jamie has never liked to talk about those early years and my obsession with spirit boards. She told me she watched me go from a polo-shirt-wearing, short-haired guy from a rich school to a long-haired hippy who loved heavy metal and fast cars. In retrospect, I did change. As I described earlier, I developed a severe anxiety disorder and had crazy panic attacks. On several occasions, I very nearly lost my life.

I know it's absolutely insane that after all I witnessed and experienced, I continued to get back on spirit boards over and over again. That feeling of adrenalin and mystery haunts me even now. It has not been easy reliving the stories for this book. I have spent years getting them all together. Multiple computer crashes and unfortunate events have again and again plagued me through the years. For a while, I gave up on the thought of telling my story.

Today I am still living in Tulsa, and pretty much living a normal life. I have met an amazing woman who does not tempt me into getting back into the dark side. I continue to respond to people who contact me with their Zozo encounters. The creepy stories and cases continue to stream in. I am currently in talks with a private filmmaker about making a documentary that focuses on my experiences, and those that have been reported all over the world in connection with what has become known as the Zozo Phenomenon.

On that cloudy day I talked to Jamie, I asked her if she would ever get back on the board with me. She gave me that disappointed look I had seen so many times before.

"Darren, somehow we unlocked something ancient and evil with that board, and I am not about to attract it back into my life," she responded. Jamie has since remarried and has had another child, whom she is still raising.

I wish I had made that same decision that she did, when she ended our marriage—to put the evil far behind.

I still could not let the opportunity go. Before she walked away, I placed a cigarette pack on the table in front of us. It was the size of a planchette. I put my fingers on it and said, "C'mon, Jamie, let's just see what happens. I gotta know."

She took a deep breath and thought about it. She reached over and gently put her fingers next to mine. Without another breath, the cigarette pack began circling around forcefully with amazing speed. We both removed our hands. Neither one of us said a word. We didn't have to. A gust of wind blew against our faces. We knew.

As Jamie walked away from me, I wondered what my life would have been like had I made the decision to not involve myself with the unseen world. Is Zozo still attached to me, waiting to surface in some unknown attack? It's a question that haunts me every day.

# 8

# Unexpected Hauntings

On the heels of the *Ghost Adventures* episode, a major film entitled *Ouija* was released on October 24, 2014. The Ouija has enjoyed enormous popularity throughout its 125-year history, but never more than in 2014, with so much media attention focused upon it. The film, backed by Hasbro, Inc., the owner and manufacturer of the Ouija, was made on a rather modest budget of five million dollars. Anticipation was high, and the audience delivered. The film debuted at number one and earned nearly $20 million on its opening weekend alone. It was released in five international markets, earning $42.7 million by its second weekend. In the United Kingdom, the film earned $2.2 million on its opening weekend, which made it the second-biggest opening weekend for a horror film to that date, behind *Annabelle*.

Although critics frowned at *Ouija*, the film seemed to move by its own direction and wound up making around $98 million dollars, despite negative reviews. And, like the board itself, it was marketed to a young audience. They did not disappoint. At one point in the film, an elderly character warns, "Do not go seeking answers from the dead," but this advice naturally goes unheeded by the young in both the film *and* in reality.

Researchers from the search engine giant Google examined search insights from Google Consumer Surveys and the top trending purchases on Google Express to determine what the most popular toys were leading up to the 2014 holiday season. The Ouija board came in fifth, undoubtedly propelled by the momentum of the film.

Searches for Ouija boards increased by 300 hundred percent, with young adults using smart phones to check prices. The Ouija was listed on various sites as one of the hottest gifts. Santa Claus's sleigh must have been loaded down with Ouijas that year, delivering them alongside other favored toys.

As I anticipated, Zozo cases spiked before, during, and after the holiday season. Thousands of comments about Zozo filtered through Twitter by usage of hashtags. I began to doubt my decision years ago to go public with my research, as now the Zozo Phenomenon had reached heights I never dreamed possible. Did I create a monster in a digital age—or just expose one to the light of day?

Spirit boards are marketed as games for fun and entertainment. Strangely, some people think this is some deliberate scheme to sell the board to the unwary. However, throughout its most of its history, the Ouija has always been considered a game. That designation comes courtesy of the IRS and, by default, the United States Supreme Court.

In the early part of the twentieth century, there were multiple manufacturers of talking boards, competing for a growing market. The Baltimore Talking Board Company maintained that the board was a "spiritual" device, and therefore tax-exempt. The IRS disagreed, and levied taxes on board manufacturers. In 1920, the Baltimore Talking Board Company took the matter to court, arguing that the board was not a game. They lost, and appealed their case all the way to the Supreme Court. The court dismissed their suit without hearing, leaving the IRS free to tax the boards as games.

The Ouija has passed through several ownerships over the past century-plus. Few official comments are ever made about the board. The present owner, Hasbro, Inc., has reaffirmed the board's status as a game for "fun and entertainment."

Many users do treat spirit boards as games that provide amusement and entertainment. They use them over and over, and nothing bad ever happens. Much of the time, nothing meaningful at all happens. There are no negative phenomena, and no ill effects linger after the board is put away.

Many others treat the board as a serious tool for opening the door to the spirit realm. The spirit board certainly can do that. Some of these types of users want to contact the dead, spirits, and even—for thrill-seeking—a demon. This faction of the board audience is made up heavily of young people, from pre-teens to college-age and twenties. Many of them secretly hope for a dramatic experience comparable to the movies, something to show off to their friends and enhance their peer status.

Those who are most vulnerable to a Zozo-style experience are young users, who are immature, easily scared, and often desirous of copy-catting Hollywood. Older, more experienced users can also encounter Zozo, however, and sometimes they are blind-sided. Beginners and less experienced persons of any age can run into Zozo, too.

Zozo often seems to be attracted to people who are experiencing depression, and who are lonely and vulnerable. Teenagers and pre-teens, whose emotions are often on a roller coaster, are likely to be the ones most affected by this disturbing phenomenon. Even taking into consideration that teenagers may secretly want to be scared, and also may embellish, their experiences are still disturbing. As one who has researched board phenomena for a number of years now, I have received hundreds of emails from teens and pre-teens who have played the board as a game. I have also heard from their concerned parents. Here are a few stories from my archives, used with permission.

## The touching entity

In this account, a teenager suffers post-board phenomena that she attributes to Zozo:

> I wanted to share this account to discourage others from messing with this kind of stuff. I'm sixteen, and several months ago before school started, my friend and I decided to use her glow in the dark board, the first time we ever dared to do it in her room. We had done it before plenty of times with only a single "bad" session.

It started out simply enough, with only a few things slightly alarming us, like when we could tell that the entity was clearly lying (when we asked it if it had been human before, for example.) It then started to hesitate answering almost every question we asked, and moving in several figure eights each time.

It answered rather quickly and without hesitation when we asked its name, immediately spelling out ZOZO.

I stupidly asked it if it wanted something from either of us. It said YES. We both asked it if it wanted something from us individually, and it said it didn't want something from her, but from me. I asked it what it wanted, and before I had finished the question, it moved in several figure eights and spelled out MINE. I asked it if it meant it had just claimed me, what it wanted with me, and why it wanted me, and it refused to say anything but MINE quickly, over and over again. We got really scared so we asked if we could leave and it pointed to YES before the cursor shot off of the board and across the room.

All night I couldn't sleep because I kept feeling hands touching my ankles and pulling on my feet, almost as if something was messing with me, just trying to scare me. The worst part was feeling the light scratching of the clawed fingers and getting up the next morning to red, irritated lines running down my legs.

As I said before, it's been several months since we used the board, and at some point every night, I can feel something touching me, and occasionally it pinches me and leaves marks for me to find the next morning. I have tried many, many things to get rid of it. Trust me when I say you should *not* play with boards, or at least leave as soon as the board starts to spell a Z when you ask for the entity's name.

Update: Also thought I should share a few more things that happened after my initial email. I never did seek professional help, and eventually everything stopped on its own, thankfully, but not before a few more things happened. I started to think everything was okay after the scratches stopped, but for a few weeks I began to wake up at exactly two-thirty in the morning with my blankets on the floor. The first time I woke up, I didn't think much of it until I grabbed them and found that they were still warm like they had just been on me, but they were far enough away that it would have taken me a long time to kick them all that way. I still dismissed it until it started happening every night. After a while, that stopped, too.

My friend later offered to give me her Ouija board. Since everything had stopped by then, I half convinced myself none of it had happened and accepted. I decided to keep it in a black bag in my closet because I read that the only way to get rid of one was to put it in one [a black bag] and bury it, so I thought that would be the safest way to keep it.

A couple months went by and I had gotten the Ouija board out again because some of my friends wanted to play. However, we took it out of the bag and decided not to play because I had told them what had happened before, and we all got too scared. I set it on my floor and completely forgot about it until my friends had left and I had gone to bed.

I was leaning over my bed in the dark to plug in my phone charger when I heard my name shouted in my ear in a male voice. I screamed and jumped back onto my bed. I was absolutely terrified all night and didn't get any sleep because I was home alone. I finally got up the next morning when my mom came home and realized that the board was halfway out of the bag right where I had heard the voice. I zipped it back up in the bag, buried it under boxes in my closet, and I haven't taken it out since then.

As a parent, I do not think I would want my teenage daughter having such thoughts regardless if I believed in spirits or not! It seems this game can bring about a lot more than innocent fun!

## Reign of terror

A young man from France describes the terrible fallout from an unexpected encounter with Zozo. The translation is as it was received:

Here is, word by word, what happened to me. I swear that this story is real and it is not a question of "collective hallucination." My story happened at the end of June, 2006, when I was nineteen.

One night, my aunt and my cousins invite me to dinner and sleep at their house. At this moment, I felt bad because my first love and I broke up. We eat, we drink (too much I think), and watch a DVD. My aunt goes to bed, also does my cousin. I'm alone with my seventeen-year-old cousin in the living room.

"Well, what are we doing?"

"Hmmmm, do you get [have] a Ouija board?"

"Oh, yes I do! Let's do play to pass the time."

Before the seance, I've already done some seances and it really had impress me!

My cousin and I were a bit drunk (whiskey coke). We started to play, lights on (we already said a prayer and light two white candles). We did not think that Ouija could work with two persons playing on it.

"Is there anybody here?" We heard the table crackling.

"Can you tell us your name?" No response.

Few minutes later, a spirit come and had predict the death of my cousin, in a bike accident, he gave us dates...He told us that he was in the room and that he saw us through the eyes of the "fox terrier" (dog).

Sometimes the planchette went off the board.

We gently asked the entity to leave us.

A moment later, I asked to talk to my grandfather, dad's side, who passed away five years earlier, from a lung cancer. The only response we received was, "Bark on my grave!"

I asked, "Grandpa, if you're there, can you prove it one way or another?

Ten seconds without a response, and suddenly I feel like I'm not myself...My cousin is sitting next to me, on my right side, he touches my arm and BAM I receive an electroshock. My head falls on the side, and I don't know how, my necklace (a Christian cross) starts to levitate...!!! As if someone was trying to get it off of my neck...Ten seconds pass, it stops, and my cousin, terrorized, look at me and say "Oh my God, your eyes are black! There's no white!!!!

I puke few seconds later, and my cousin felt he needed to continue the "game." He put his hands on the planchette, ask if there's anybody with us, and wait...few seconds pass and the planchette starts to move, slowly, and spell ZOZOZO, it goes to the letter three times in a row. We did not know anything about this demon, nor about any "renown" demons by the way!! My cousin was afraid, I was sick and sad, without energy in me...my cousin continues to ask questions.

"Who are you?" It spelled ZOZO again.

"Are you a good spirit?" YES.

"What do you want to us?" It spelled the letters S and E and stopped.

"What does mean SE?" It spelled SEX.

My cousin looked at me and the planchette continues to move, spelling the words KILL, FUCK, SUFFER.

We decided to stop the session, forgetting to thank the entities.

I do not know if it's because of this mistake, but since this session, our lives are like hell!!! We have frequently car accidents, we're always sick, sometimes mad at people without knowing why. My cousin tried two times to commit suicide. I don't know what to do, I'm scared.

## Red eyes from Down Under

The next one comes from Australia. The family brought in the services of a well-known, ex-law enforcement chaplain who had retired and began a career performing exorcisms. While I cannot provide details of the ordeal, I have been granted permission to share the first email from one of the teenage sisters:

I came across your website earlier today, when my sister told me the name of what is in our house. Although much was happening beforehand, I was silly enough to try out a Oujia board afterwards, although I thought I closed it off properly. However, despite that I'm only sixteen, I'm aware of the consequences. When my fourteen-year-old sister told me today that Zozo was what was in our house, I had a flashback to receiving messages from the board, and I remember that name came up.

I'm now worried about it. My family is very in tune to all spiritual phenomena, and have experienced a lot. My mum especially has experienced a demonic presence since she was little. But it came back after I did the board. She said that there was a talon sticking into her back whilst she was sleeping and a demonic laugh was breathed into her ear.

I've experienced various supernatural things throughout my life, but not of the demonic nature, until last night. I was in a dream state of sleep when I heard an evil breathing right in my ear. It was super loud and I ran out my room straight away into my mum's bed. I never get scared like that, but I truly heard it.

I then laid in my mum's bed, but stayed awake, as I could feel the uneasy presence watching us. My mum then got up for the toilet, although she said to me this morning she was scared....and she never gets scared as she always faces it, but then returns shutting my door. About five minutes later, we heard this loud cat-like screech, but it was almost not a cat, as none come near our house.

My mum is visiting a priest on Monday, but also when emailing him, her computer crashed twice. Before that happened last night, an hour earlier my fourteen-year-old sister said that there was a six-foot dark shadow standing at the end of her bed watching her with red eyes. Please can you help! I fear for my family, as I feel as though it is getting worse. I'd appreciate your advice.

## Volcanic devil painting

In this account, Zozo threatens to haunt and follows up, with phenomena that reminded me of my swinging Jesus painting in the Oklahoma City house:

When I was fifteen, some friends of mine got really into the idea of Ouija. Not coming from a religious family, I thought it was a joke so I played along. I remember sitting in a friend's basement the first night we sat down to try it. It was a dark room with cement walls and no windows. The only light was from two neon black lights mounted on opposite walls. This made for a very "spooky atmosphere" and I was loving it. I wasn't scared at all but my friends were taking it so seriously.

I remember when the planchette started moving. I cracked a smile. I didn't necessarily think they were playing a trick on me, judging by their reactions, but I thought we were all collectively moving it, which felt like you were just following it across the board.

Anyway, we asked it all the usual stuff, I guess. Sometimes we got interesting answers. Sometimes something completely incoherent. Then we asked who we were speaking with. Without hesitation it spelled out ZOZO.

I laughed. It just all seemed so ridiculous.

Then it spelled something like WILL HAUNT WILL HAUNT. At this point, it had been a couple hours and we were getting bored of it.

Then my friends insisted we asked it to show itself. We asked over and over, "Show us you are real," and "Prove it."

The planchette began moving in a swift figure-eight motion. It repeated this pattern for several seconds and then the two black lights in the room began to shut on and off opposite each other.

This scared the living hell out of me. I was up and out of that room in the blink of an eye.

Of course we speculated on what happened for several days following before we lost interest.

Then a few weeks later something truly bizarre happened to me which I still think about thirteen years later.

My father has been an artist his whole life. Growing up, there were always paintings around the house he had done.

I remember my grandmother gave me one he had done when he was fourteen or fifteen years old. It was a painting of an erupting volcano on the horizon. In the foreground was a devil, trident in hand, sprawled out on his behind next to a lifeless tree. My dad explained that the volcano spit the devil out from hell and now here he was, next to this tree, lost and confused. This painting struck me as so funny. So I had in sitting in my bedroom window at my parents' house.

Well, on that day several weeks after the Ouija incident, I came home from school in the afternoon and my bedroom door wouldn't open, which was odd because it had no lock. I shook the handle with no luck. So I kicked in the door to get in. I didn't break it off its hinges but broke through whatever was blocking it. I surveyed the room.

A shelf had fallen off the wall and jammed itself between the door and one of my big 1970s stereo speakers, blocking the door. Candles, toys, and whatever junk I had on the shelf were spread out across the floor where the shelf had fallen.

I looked at my bed and saw my dad's painting, which had been in the window on the opposite side of the room, was now laying right on my pillow.

My heart sank. I remember being so terrified. I asked my parents if they knew anything about it and they acted like I was crazy.

I told my friends with the Ouija board and they were hysterical. Looking back on it, it's pretty funny, actually.

It sparked a stint of three to four weekends of more Ouija. All of which were uneventful. I do remember one of them saying they read online that ZOZO was supposed to be some demon, but I never looked into it too much myself.

We quickly lost interest and moved on to other things. Nothing weird ever happened again but I never forgot, and we would still mention ZOZO from time to time over the years.

I'm still not convinced it was supernatural. Maybe just coincidence. Just kids getting excited over scary stuff. But I have been reading up on paranormal phenomena lately and thought I'd search ZOZO. Anyway, I found your site, and was pretty intrigued.

Hope you find my experiences interesting.

## Paradise

I noted previously that in my own experiences, Zozo would tell females it wanted to take them to paradise. When asked where paradise was the entity would always spell HELL. This has been repeated in scores of experiences with Zozo. Here is one example from a female teenager:

I am fifteen years old and my friend and I have been contacted by this Zozo many times. We never really believed in Ouija boards, so my friend, Greta, bought one to try it out. At first, the plachette moved very slowly and only spelled out gibberish stuff.

One day, we were at a friend's house and he wanted to try to play. He had a framed whiteboard and we decided to make our own Ouija board on the cardboard back of it and use a bottle cap [as the planchette]. This time, our "planchette" moved very fast. We asked what its name was and it said ZOZO. It kept spelling out Z-O-Z-O-Z-O over and over again until we got scared and said goodbye. We were really freaked out because we all felt an eerie presence.

Me and Greta decided to Google stuff about Ouija boards and rules if you got a bad spirit... then we came across a page of articles about ZOZO. We had no clue that others had contacted the same thing that we did.

We started to get more interested in it, so we played again. We asked him where he lived and he said

PARADISE. We asked where paradise was and he said
HELL. We then asked why he contacted us and he spelt
out WEAK SOUL. This really creeped us out so we said
goodbye. Instead of going to goodbye, it started moving
in a figure eight and counting down the numbers. We
saw on some article about Ouija boards that if a spirit
counts down numbers then it could escape the board.
We screamed for it to leave and when it got to #2, it
moved very quickly to GOODBYE. As soon as we took
our fingers off of the bottle cap, the framing around our
makeshift board broke off. The room got really cold and
we all were terrified.

After playing a few more times over the next two
months, we learned that ZOZO wants Greta to give birth
to a child. He also said he rapes her and wants to give
her a baby because she is "pure." He said that on April
13 (which we found out today that it is Friday the 13th),
he was going to put a baby inside of her. She is really
creeped out and doesn't know whether or not to believe
it or what to do.

Weird things have been happening ever since we
played and we just want them to stop. Zozo threatened
to hurt my boyfriend and my little sister if we stopped
playing. We haven't played in a month, but things still
seem creepy and random things like doors opening are
still happening. Do you have any advice for us?

There is no substance to the belief that counting down the
board numbers enables a spirit to "escape" the board. Hostile spirits
can attach to people, but it is through an energetic connection that they
are able to make.

## Noisy spirit

A lark on a spirit board turned serious in this next account. Zozo uses a
zero instead of the O to spell its name:

Hi there, my name is Lynne and I live in Wisconsin. My
friend Penny actually emailed you last night regarding my

situation, and you responded by advising to cleanse the house, or to call in a priest. I'd first like to just share with you, briefly, of my recent experiences.

I moved into my current place back in May. A friend had already been living there and in October she moved out. In that same month after she left, a male friend had bought me a Ouija board (one of those glow in the dark ones). We decided to use it one night at my house, and my friend did substantial research prior to our session. We lit white candles and placed them at the corners of the board and even burned sage incense. too.

After a few minutes, we started getting responses. First we spoke with a woman named Edna and she said she was fifty-four when she passed. Then we spoke with a girl named Samantha who was eight when she passed. I can't remember the transition to Zozo, but all of a sudden the planchette started going back and forth between the Z and the number 0. It went back and forth maybe two times before my friend moved the pointer over GOODBYE and flipped the pointed upside down.

My friend looked super freaked out and informed me that while doing research, he found that Zozo is a negative entity, but didn't say much more. I got a little scared, but eventually didn't think much of it, and I haven't touched the Ouija board since.

In the past two months, there have been unexplainable events in my house. It started with noises, but not house noises like the heater kicking on or leaky pipe noises. At night time I could hear the carpet moving— as if someone placed their hand lightly over the carpet and moved it back and forth. When I heard that noise, I got up and shut my bedroom door.

The next morning when I woke up, I went in the living room and my incense holder thing was flipped around on the table. Around the same time, I noticed something else. I have a floor lamp in my living room that collects dust at the base. One day I looked and it was as if someone took their finger and drew lines that intersect in the middle, where the pole is. I drew a line next to one of them, and my finger is way slimmer than the existing marks.

Last week a friend and I got back from shopping and the locks on my back door were all unlocked: chain, latch, and door knob. I know for a fact all three were locked before I left, I had done laundry and remember locking the latch and chain. I never unlock the doorknob either.

Yesterday, my thermostat changed. It's the old mercury kind with a dial, top half is what you set the temp to and the bottom half is the actual temp. I had set the temp to sixty-five degrees and then I went out to shovel. This was in the afternoon. About fifteen minutes later I came back in and was just sitting around for a while. I walked past the thermostat and noticed that it had been turned and set to forty degrees. All this last week for no reason at all, I get reallllly nervous/scared at night. Not sure if it's a "I know someone's watching me" feeling, but it's very uneasy.

Anyway, those occurrences are unexplainable to me. After my roommate moved out, my landlord changed the locks on the door, and he's the only one with a key to my place. He's also handicapped and can't get around by himself. I'm the only person in my house.

Do you think that everything that has happened is because of the Ouija board? I think calling in a priest or "cleansing" the house is a bit extreme, as I'm still in the early process of trying to figure everything out. Do you recommend trying to figure out what exactly is going on? Or should I just ignore it? And how would I know for sure that what I'm dealing with is indeed a bad spirit?

There is enough going on in this house to warrant a cleansing, as the phenomena could be related to the "lingering effects" hat accompany Zozo manifestations.

## The alien hand

Zozo is attracted to females, especially between the ages of twelve and thirty, in a perverse sexual manner. Some victims have reported sexual encounters against their will. One woman in North Carolina reported to me that after having Zozo surface on a spirit board, she locked herself in a closet and developed an alien hand syndrome where she lost physical control and performed acts on herself. This experience left her very troubled to the point that she made the drive all the way to Oklahoma City where I was residing at the time. She revealed to me that Zozo had given her a message to kill me during an automatic writing session. She showed me the actual piece of paper that chillingly spelled KILL DARREN. This of course raised an eyebrow with me, reminding me of the same message delivered by the board in my experiences in Michigan. I must say I was quite rattled by this woman's story.

Skeptics have dismissed Zozo as a recent board phenomenon created by mass hysteria and copycat self-fulfillment. My research revealed that references to Zozo go back many centuries. It appears Zozo has been around for a very long time, lying in wait, making mischief, creating havoc, and nearly destroying lives—as it nearly destroyed mine.

# Part II
# Unmasking Zozo

Darren Evans and Rosemary Ellen Guiley go down the rabbit hole looking for evidence that reveals the true nature of Zozo. They find bizarre and intriguing connections—and more mystery than ever.

# 9

## The Z-Entities

Zozo operates under a variety of names, yet the characteristics of the encounters clearly point to the same entity. Zozo especially uses different Z names, including simply the letter Z, as well as Zo, Za, Zaza, Zam, Zepot, Z8, Zono and more. The Z alternates are so frequent that Darren dubbed them the "Z-entities," for all of them seem to be alter egos of the same massive ego displayed by Zozo.

### Gender bender
Most experiencers refer to Zozo in masculine gender, but some instinctively feel that Zozo is a "she." The more likely answer is a neutral "it," but Zozo has obvious shapeshifting ability to blur its identity and make the right impressions on victims. From a young woman:

> I'm writing reluctantly, because I don't know if I want to know anymore. Is it possible that Zozo is a woman? A group of us were "playing" and I thought it was my best

friend going back and forth between the Z and the O trying to scare me. Then we heard a very loud bang and my dog mysteriously disappeared out of our yard through a locked gate.

Since that, in that house, my younger daughter, four to five years old at the time, would see things. A woman with long greasy hair walking in front of my bedroom dressed in all black (long dress), people in costumes hiding in her closet, etc. Normally, I would pass this off as childhood imagination. However, I began to have disturbing dreams reciting "The Lord's Prayer" in my sleep. In my dreams, I kept forgetting the words, when I know them well. I've moved three times since then and still have these dreams. Very disturbing, very real.

It's been ten years and my daughter still swears there was somebody "walking" through the house. I've also received texts from my best friend who encountered Zozo frequently (the person who got me on the board to begin with), saying that she's "Zozo." She was almost obsessed at times with this. When I asked her about it, she had no idea what I was talking about. She got very upset when I mentioned it. She had an experience and will not tell me everything that happened when she would frequently talk to this "thing." I don't even like to mention the name.

Is any of this related? Is this thing a woman? Could it be following me? I've moved halfway across the country and still wonder. No spectacular occurrences compared to what I've read, but scary for me.

Scary is right—all of these things are interrelated in the complex phenomenon of Zozo: different names, both genders, and a host of unpleasant side effects, many of which continue after board use has stopped The Z-entities may be decoys to fool unwary users.

## Z calling

Zozo often prefers the shorthand of the letter Z. If board players are not familiar with Zozo, they will not automatically know who Z is and will

continue communicating, thus risking giving Zozo a stronger connection
to them. Here are some examples:

> My aunt and I played a Ouija board four years ago. It
> started out simple enough... rambling letters that didn't
> make real words. When I asked for a name, all it gave us
> was the letter Z. It continued to ramble weird spellings. It
> continued to tell me that it was a male, he was killed in
> 1869 by being stabbed in the neck with a piece of glass.
> He said he was buried to the left of the picnic table and
> that he wanted us to dig. There happen to be two picnic
> tables, one in my aunt's yard and one in her mother-in-
> law's yard. We asked my aunt's sister-in-law the next
> day about it. Indeed, there was a hump in the ground, a
> mound of earth, to the left of their picnic table. We had no
> intention of digging this guy up if he was there, for fear of
> what we would find and what we would unleash.
>     Months later we played again. Z came through
> again. He said he liked children. I asked him what he
> liked to do with children. It spelled KIL, then an explosion
> lit up the night sky in the mobile home park. We were
> startled, we both let go of the planchette without closing
> and ran outside. The neighbor was burning trash and an
> aerosol can just happen to get tossed in there. However,
> the coincidence of timing was disturbing to me. We put it
> up for the night.
>     The next morning there were shards of sharp
> glass on the ground under the kitchen window, the room
> where we had been playing. A few weeks later we played
> again. Yet again Z came through. The board spelled out
> MASON, the last name of two surviving members of our
> matriarch line. I asked which Mason it referred to...M it
> said. My great grandmother's name was M____ Mason,
> at the time she was ninety-five. It went on to explain that
> she would die in her rest. I asked when, it simply said
> THREE. My aunt couldn't take anymore. We quit. [On]
> October 13 of the same year, M____ Mason died at 3 PM.
>     Everywhere I move, strange things happen. Now,
> mind you, I have had spiritual experiences since the age

of four and seeing that it didn't seem to be negative I paid it no attention. Until I found shards of sharp glass on the ground underneath mine and my new fiance's bedroom window. I immediately went to a local spiritual supply store and bought some white sage incense. I blessed the house, paying attention to all windows and doors. The energy seemed to lighten and my mind was at ease.

Little did I know that the Ouija board remained in my aunt's possession. She has since been diagnosed with multiple psychiatric disorders. A couple of months after our first initial contact with Z, I was diagnosed as being bipolar.

This new home of ours is...strange. I thought I had gotten rid of the negative energy. However, the day I moved in here I was attacked by two females in a parking lot while I was shopping for the new home. I stopped going to college and work.

I made a new friend out here who can see spirits, I can only sense them. For some reason, we had a seance in my bathroom. We sensed and saw a little boy's shadow drowning in my garden tub. We heard a growling noise coming from my hallway. LP [friend] got scratched on the ankle. We closed and quit. We were sitting in my living room when LP said he saw a white mist moving down my hallway. I looked and saw a face in my bedroom doorway (I thought the door was open because I couldn't see the door knob.). The face that I saw was white with black eyes, black nostrils, black mouth and a black hat. I had seen a similar face in a dream I had two weeks before M___ Mason passed away. I recognized it to be an angel of death. I told LP this. He went home and received the call that his grandma had just died of a sudden heart attack while attending a night club with LP's mother.

I have changed the energy of this house by taking tips from a book. While it has helped, the tension in my life hasn't ceased. I had an anxiety attack, I ended up kicking two neighbors out of my car after a paranormal investigation on Halloween night. I have been raped twice since the start of my Z experience, been beat up three times, I can't keep a job, and my husband got punched in the face. My aunt threw the Ouija board away because weird things were happening in her house. We have to move again because this neighborhood has gone downhill since summer's end.

I don't know what to do or how to get rid of "Z." After seeing your [Darren's] debut on *Ghost Adventures*, I began my own research. Turns out Zozo can and has represented himself to others with just the letter Z. That's when everything came into focus. So, yea, that's my Z story. Thank you for taking the time to read this. Blessed be.

Here is another case of lingering bad effects after appearances by Z:

It started when I was about thirteen, and two friends and I decided to play the Ouija board. We didn't own one, so we figured we'd just make one. We used a piece of cardboard from a box, a Sharpie to write the letters and numbers, and a small shot glass as the planchette. We sat upstairs in one of the guest bedrooms, just the three of us in the house. Keep in mind this was the middle of the day, and so it was fairly bright outside and in the room.

We sat around the board, excited and nervous at the same time. We each placed one finger very lightly on the top of the shot glass, and we began asking questions. "Is anyone here with us?" "Can you hear us?" We didn't get any activity for quite some time.

Then something happened. The planchette began to move, but the answers it was giving us did not make any sense. It just moved all around the board, as if it was trying to figure out what to say. "Who are you? Give us your name." We asked the spirit to identify itself.

The planchette quickly shot over to the letter Z. The three of us looked at each other...that's strange, we were all thinking. We asked this spirit Z what year it died. It answered loosely, "1908." After the name and year, none of the other answers made sense again. We began to get a little irritated with this spirit and decided to clear out the board by running the planchette over the "Goodbye" word and saying out loud, "Okay. We'd like to talk to someone else now, so goodbye."

We stopped playing with the Ouija board and went downstairs to watch some TV for a while. Surely we'll get a different spirit the next time we go up and play with it, we all said. So after a few hours, we decided to run up the steps and play with the Ouija board again. As soon as we began talking to it, the spirit talking to us kept running over the letter Z. Constantly to the letter Z, the planchette would move. We began getting a little freaked out at this point, and tried clearing the board again. But each time we played, the same spirit would talk to us... spelling out random unidentifiable words and pausing over the Z time and time again.

The air in the room was thick and heavy, and the three of us were frightened. Why couldn't we get rid of this spirit? Why is he hanging around like an unwelcome guest?

After tossing the board and planchette into the trash, my friends went home and I was left to experience the frightening things going on in my house. Loud footsteps at night, doors opening and shutting by themselves, and strange voices emanating from the shadows. My brother even swore that he heard someone breathing under his bed one night. When we moved, the hauntings stopped... did this spirit Z hang around to mess with us?

This pattern of behavior repeats in case after case. Zozo's impact does sometimes linger long after board use has stopped, as many of the stories in this book show.

## Who was Alan Vaughan's Z?

Zozo may have shown up as early as 1965 as Z, manifesting to the famous psychic, Alan Vaughan. In his book *Patterns of Prophecy* (1966), Vaughan described his experiences.

Vaughan, born in 1936, did not realize he had psychic ability until he used a Ouija board. In November 1965, he bought a board to amuse a friend who was convalescing, and they began using the board on November 5.

On November 8, newspaper columnist Dorothy Kilgallen, also a popular television personality, was reported dead of a heart attack. Vaughan and his friend asked the board if that manner of death was true, and the board answered that she had been poisoned. Ten days later, an inquest into her death revealed poisoning as the cause. (Many believed that Kilgallen had been murdered because she knew the truth of President John F. Kennedy's assassination.)

Then a board spirit named NADA ("nothing" in Spanish) pushed its way into Vaughan's head. Vaughan said, I could hear her voice repeating the same phrases over and over again."

He asked the board about this, and the answer was, AWFUL CONSEQUENCES—POSSESSION. Wrote Vaughan, "At that point I became alarmed, for it had not occurred to me that having a strange voice in one's head was tantamount to possession."

A friend who was knowledgeable about spirits tried to help Vaughan, but another entity that called itself Z pushed into head as well. Z took possession of Vaughan's hand and made him write out a message: "Each of us has a spirit while living. Do not meddle with the spirits of the dead."

Vaughan said:

As I wrote out this message I began to feel an energy rising up in my body and entering my brain. It pushed out both "Nada" and "Z." My friends noted that my face, which had been white and pinched, suddenly flooded with color. I felt a tremendous sense of elation and physical wellbeing.

What this mysterious force was, Vaughan did not say. But after his "self-exorcism," he realized he had marked psychic abilities, especially precognition, the ability to see the future. He became famous for many of his predictions.

Who was Z? The answer is not known. It was an entity or force strong enough to invade Vaughan's mind and take control of his body.

The message about the "awful consequences" of possession was accurate, however. If a person becomes obsessed with using a spirit board and allows a communicating entity to lodge in the mind, a potentially dangerous threshold has been crossed.

## Other Z names

Zozo also has used the friendly-sounding name of Zeke—although its behavior is anything but friendly. Here is one account:

> I found [Darren's] blog because I was researching a spirit I had encountered December of 2009 while playing with a Ouija board. I thought I'd share with you.
>
> Our school [a university] had been shut down due to snow. My friends and I were all very bored, so we watched that movie, *Paranormal Activity*. The next day, I went out and bought a Ouija board (not the smartest decision I've ever made). We got a bunch of people to get in on it. It was thrilling. I had no idea of the events that would follow our use and how addicting it would become.
>
> My then friend, Charlotte, and one or two other people were there. We laid the board on the coffee table in the old tiny dorm room, lit some candles for some mood lighting (we were super cheesy). And we began our journey with a simple question, "Is anyone out there?" A few seconds later, as we were all becoming a little disheartened, the board piece (sorry, I don't know what it's called) began to move. We expected it to be incoherent messages, as the box said not to expect anything grandiose the first time using it. However, we struck up a conversation with a spirit. It was boring at first. He introduced himself as an old man named Zeke, didn't tell us a whole lot. But we began getting a bad feeling, so we told him we wanted to talk to someone else. He wouldn't have it. Then we watched as our board piece moved back and forth, faster than we would have expected, from H to A and back again. H-A-H-A-H-A-H-A.
>
> We stopped playing with it and moved to a different area. After that we talked to a plethora of spirits,

a coke addict in hell who loved it there because he had all the coke he wanted. He shot a guy who his girlfriend had been cheating on him with, but the other guy shot him too and aimed better. And we also had some pretty exquisite experiences where we spoke to some spirits who claimed to be our guardian angels. They couldn't see each other, they explained the whole process to us, we learned some very life changing things, but they always left us with a warning, "you have to stop."

Later, after we had been playing with it for a few days, in the middle of talking to another spirit we get H-A-H-A-H-A-H-A again. We asked if it was the name of the spirit we were talking to previously and it just kept spelling H-A-H-A-H-A-H-A. These kind of occurrences became regular and we learned to just tell him to go away and he'd leave us alone.

One night, we were playing with the Ouija board again, with Charlotte, her boyfriend at the time, and another friend of ours. The time spent at the Ouija board was not memorable, but I do remember Charlotte complaining of being fatigued, so she laid down on the couch. Everyone else went about their business, and it took about fifteen minutes, but finally her boyfriend realized that she hadn't moved since she laid down, but her eyes were wide open. We tried talking to her and she wouldn't respond. He asked her if she wanted any water and when she didn't respond he asked again. She replied, very snarkily, that no, she didn't want water. I got up because I was thirsty and headed to the kitchen. When I was half way there, she said, "I want some water!" and stood up and walked to the kitchen. The crazy part is, she did so faster than I've ever seen a person walk. Like someone just clicked fast forward. She beat me to the kitchen. I didn't know what to say. Forty-five minutes later she came out of her stupor, apologizing for falling asleep. We all looked at her warily but decided to let it go.

Then, one afternoon, in between classes, which had started up again, we decided to pull it [the board] out because we had an extra-long break. Immediately it was "Zeke" again, who told us his name wasn't Zeke but when we asked what his real name was, he just laughed again. Suddenly, in the middle of his laugh, the piece flew off the board in Charlotte's direction. Startled, we all let out a squeal and then a nervous laugh. But Charlotte didn't stop laughing. She threw her head back, hysterical, and she had a look in her eyes that wasn't her own. Almost immediately, Vanessa and I were worried. We tried to touch her but she flinched away from our hands, burying herself as deep into the chair as possible. We finally were able to touch her and she stopped, looked at us, and broke out crying, bawling her eyes out, then in another split second, almost too fast for our brains to process, she jerked her hand away and was once again laughing, pulled up into the chair.

Vanessa grabbed her, wrapped her arms around Charlotte, pinning her arms to her side, and began to pray, Charlotte writhing in her hold. I prayed too, silently, though Vanessa swears she could hear me. Finally, Charlotte went limp, crying on Vanessa's shoulder, Vanessa whispering for her to calm down, rocking her. When she had finally cooled down, she told us that she didn't really understand what was going on, all she remembered was crying, and then she would black out.

Things happened to me as well, such as pounding on the bathroom door while showering and no one else hearing it, scratches on my arm, and much later than that, after I had moved and become pregnant, dark entities in my bedroom hovering over me. I am fairly certain that Zozo was the one who we had talked to and who had possessed Charlotte. I'm not even sure she's free of a demonic hold, even now. She has travelled a dark road, seeking popularity, she wants to be worshipped, it seems, and has made a joy out of stealing husbands. I have since stopped talking to her. But you can see in her pictures, she doesn't have the right look in her eye anymore. Oh, and she completely denies the possessions ever happening. (that is, unless it can bring her more attention). Thank you.

The use of Zeke—a nickname for Zechariah—brings up questions about a famous Ouija story from the 1990s involving American soldiers who went AWOL after listening to board spirits with Biblical names, including Zechariah. Here is the story:

## The Gulf Breeze 6

Did a Z-entity help to influence a group of American soldiers to go AWOL in order to combat the end of the world? The case of the "Gulf Breeze 6" defies logic—like many cases in the paranormal and ufology fields.

In 1990, the news media reported that six U.S. Army intelligence analysts deserted their military posts in West Germany because spirits talking through a Ouija advised them they were needed elsewhere in the world to lead humanity through impending cataclysms. The soldiers ranged in age from nineteen to twenty-seven years of age.

The soldiers were stationed in Augsburg, West Germany, where they all had top secret security clearances with the National Security Agency (NSA) in the 701st Military Intelligence Brigade. In November 1989, they decided to experiment to see if there was any validity to extra-sensory perception, ghosts, and other paranormal phenomena. Nothing happened until they tried a Ouija board. The soldiers communicated with several spirits, all of whom gave Biblical names, who predicted the Gulf War and the 1990 Iran earthquake, and issued dire doomsday warnings.

In May 1990, the spirits told the soldiers that they should get out of the military because serious things were going to happen over the next five years. "Being in the service would not help us grow and become what we were supposed to come," according to one of the six. They were further told by the spirits that they were destined to teach and prepare people for the "coming chaos," which would include Earth changes, the Second Coming of Christ, the Rapture of the faithful into heaven, and other upheavals.

The soldiers could find no way to legally get out of the Army early. The spirits told them, "Leave, just leave," and said they would be protected. So they did, on forged leave papers.

On July 3, 1990 they returned to the United States via Atlanta, and went to Chattanooga, Tennessee, where they rented a van and drove to Gulf Breeze, Florida. At the time, Gulf Breeze was a hotbed of UFO activity and sightings. It is not clear that the UFO activity was a reason to go there, but the soldiers had trained in nearby Pensacola, and had friends there.

They were arrested on July 14 when one of them was stopped for a broken tail light on his vehicle. They were taken to Fort Knox, Kentucky, for an investigation, and were held in solitary confinement. Relatives of the detainees leaked information as to the events surrounding this mysterious case, catching the attention of members of Congress. Speculation soon became rampant, and the media began asking questions, much to the embarrassment of Pentagon officials. Word spread that the soldiers were to be severely punished by full military tribunal.

Two weeks later, however, to the shock of many, they were honorably discharged instead of court martialed. Officially, it was stated that no evidence was found that they had been involved in espionage. They were reduced to the lowest rank and had to forfeit a half-month's pay.

Interviewed by the news media, one of the six predicted that every major city in the United States would soon collapse into martial law and economic chaos. He and the others would emerge to "help put the pieces back together."

The incident was much more complicated than it appeared on the surface. The leader of the group, Vance Davis, was trained in Silva Mind Control and was involved in secret psychic experiments and research while stationed at Ft. Meade, Maryland. He had studied Silva Mind Control as a teenager, and as a result was contacted by a female alien named Kia, who had green skin and said she was from a planet forty-five lights years from the Earth. Her telepathic race was coming to Earth in 1992 to help protect the planet from the end times.

It is doubtful that the Gulf Breeze 6 decided on a whim or lark to use the Ouija board. Vance was a spiritual, if not religious, person with his own eschatological views. He believed in reincarnation, and that he had been sacrificed to the gods in a previous life. Human beings are survivors of a great war, and were put on this planet and cut off from the universe. Humans have a special "Jesus gene" that cannot be copied or manipulated. The U.S. government had been in a secret relationship with aliens, of which there were two factions: the Alliance, who wanted to help humanity, and "The Others," who carried out frightening abductions and medical experiments.

So, it is no surprise that the entities who came through the board had messages catering to these interests, and had Biblical names such as Zechariah, Mark, Timothy, and even the Virgin Mary. Only one communicator did not: another female named Safire.

The board sessions last from December 1989 to July 1990, during which the spirits delivered messages of impending disaster, including a great European-U.S. conflict.

When the news story of the soldiers' desertion and arrests broke, the *Northwest Florida Daily News* had a headline that stated, "6 AWOL Soldiers Say They Aimed to Kill the Antichrist." The military investigation generated 1600 pages of documents—1400 of which were classified.

Davis wrote about the incident in his autobiography, *Unbroken Promises: A True Story of Courage and Belief*, which was published in 1995. He said he and the others became engaged in dramatic seances in which they were detailed predictions of world events, and also the arrival of the false Messiah in 1998. Some of the predictions came true, most notably an accurate death count of a major earthquake that struck Iran. At that point, the soldiers became convinced that they were really dealing with nonhuman entities, and that they had been chosen to carry out a mission for God's will. When they asked for advice how to carry out their mission to save humanity, they were told to leave their posts.

The detailed notes taken from the intense Ouija sessions were supposedly given to military officials upon their arrest.

Davis's book is full of conspiracy theories and government cover-ups—including his assertion that he had been "retrained in history," that is, events have not happened as we believe. His book has been both dismissed and described as too knowledgeable for it not to be based in truth. Many of the predictions of upheaval, war, and destruction never came to pass, however.

The effects surrounding the Gulf Breeze 6 remain perplexing and astonishing. Ufologists and others who attempted to investigate this case have speculated that government officials may have been experimenting with methods of mind control—but with Ouija boards? Was the government tampering with inter-dimensionality? Why does so much of the military investigation remain strictly classified? We may never know.

Might Zozo have used a biblical Z alter ego to cater to the interests of the soldiers?

## Oz variations

Sometimes Zozo seems to enjoy transposing letters and spelling its name backwards, such as Ozoz and Ozzo, perhaps to confound people and temporarily disguise its true identity. From a young man comes this account of OZOZ—rather chilling in that the experiencer was not working the board, but was only a spectator:

> A few years ago, I was doing some on-line research about a Ouija-board "spirit" that I encountered. I realized then, that all this time, I had been doing the wrong Google searches. For years, I've been trying to decipher the spirit's name, and what the letters mean. I could never find anything on the web about him. Since 1996, I've been looking for info about a spirit named "OZOZ." One day, I tried searching for "ZOZO." And there it was, a search result for your [Darren's] website.
>
> In short, I have witnessed this so-called spirit three times. I thought his name was OZOZ because the Ouija pointer would just move so fast, back-and-forth, from letter O to letter Z. What really scared me the most is that all three times, I was never in contact with the Ouija board or pointer. Every time this spirit came on the board, I was merely a spectator in the room. On these three separate occasions, I just was watching friends play with a Ouija board. Yet what really freaked me was that on each separate occasion, the people who were using the board (and or watching the event) were different. Meaning: In 1994, I was with some friends in my home-town, watching them play on a Ouija board. In 1995, I was in college, in a dorm-room with a totally different group of people. And in 1996 at a friend's apartment, with another entirely different set of people, the ZOZO spirit identified himself.
>
> All three times this spirit ZOZO came on the board. The first time, it scared me and I just made memory of it. The second time, I got "chills down my neck" scared. The third time made me a believer. The specifics of each account are long stories...

My life has been forever changed from these experiences. This spirit wanted ME and was very hostile. On the second and third occasions, the people who were using the board had no knowledge of my previous ZOZO encounter(s). For this reason alone, I find the whole phenomenon very disturbing.

Thanks to your research, I can see that I'm not the only one who's come across this ZOZO entity.

After Darren's appearance on *Ghost Adventures*, a brief account came in from a woman about OZZO. The description is extreme, and we were unable to verify the details. However, it follows a pattern of similar accounts:

I saw your story on *Ghost Adventures*. I almost didn't watch it...isn't it funny that those of us who have encountered this thing never want to talk about it. I had a friend in high school who was into Ouija and witchcraft. The name we got was Ozzo. Still terrifies me. She became possessed, there was a failed attempt to rid her of it, people were hurt.

She changed drastically. Became a nymphomaniac, later a prostitute. Her boyfriends died. Often. ... This thing followed me for years, until I learned to keep it out.

This all happened in 1979 in Wichita Falls. I don't know what finally happened to my friend. I do know that what you are saying is true. Good luck to you.

## Mama

One of the strangest alter egos to surface is Mama. There is no Z and no motherly love, for Mama is one of the most terrifying of the Z-entities, as these stories indicate:

I am writing to tell you of some experiences with a Ouija board my sons, nephew and I have had. We came across the MAMA or AMAMA entity... twice... in two separate places. It made no sense and both times mainly just spelled out "mamamamamamama" really, really fast... and STRONG.

> We haven't used the board in a couple of years...
> but since doing some research lately and coming across
> this phenomena, I think we will destroy the board and do
> a house smudging. The last couple of years have been
> HELL for my family and I wondered sometimes if I was
> hexed, but couldn't think of anyone at all that knew how
> to do a hex, much less would WANT to hex my family.
> Now I wonder if it is this entity causing all this havoc.
> I consider myself a "sensitive" and this particular board
> makes me uneasy every time I encounter it.
>
> I cannot even begin to tell you the horrendous
> "bad luck" my family, who have lived in this house, have
> had. Amputation, mental breakdown, financial woes,
> every vehicle we have owned in the last couple of years
> has ended up at the junkyard, illnesses, job losses, etc.
> On and on and on...

Sometimes the first communicator is Zozo or one of its Z-entity identities, who then give way to Mama. Sometimes Mama comes alone, and sometimes Zozo makes references to Mama. There are any number of permutations, as Zozo can shapeshift rapidly according to each circumstance.

Here is a case in which Zozo identifies itself as Zam and then refers to Mama as though it is a separate entity:

> My name is Sue, and I have been using the Ouija board on
> and off for about nine years with my best friend, Deanna.
> One of the only occurrences that have arrived since we
> began playing was an entity calling himself Zam. This
> spirit is frequently accompanied and/or speaks about his
> "MAMA." He constantly follows or haunts every board we
> have purchased and in every location over the years.
>
> When Zam comes through the board, the
> planchette moves incredibly faster than anything else
> we have ever encountered. ZAM tends to say disturbing
> and puzzling things. Also, we can definitely feel the
> presence moments before the planchette moves. We
> recently have decided to research our experiences with

the Ouija, and this repetitive spirit. During our research, we came upon a few websites that coincidently have the same or similar experiences, yours being one of them. Please know that nothing harmful or malicious has occurred over the years, however, we feel that you could be the most legitimate person we could turn to for some answers.

The danger in situations such as this is that the tables can turn to the negative at any time. Even though the writer insists nothing negative is going on, she admits that Zam says "disturbing and puzzling things." Zozo often starts out as a benign entity, then turns malicious when it senses the time is right. It is capable of waiting for a very long time, even years.

The most common combination of Z-entity names Mama and Zaza. Usually, Zaza comes first, then Mama. This account is from a woman named Rhonda:

I recently stumbled across your blog while I was researching occurrences that I encountered while using the Ouija board. It started several months ago much like many of the other stories. My boyfriend bought a Ouija board because he was interested in using it. I tried to be cautious and researched proper ways to close sessions. I also came across the Zozo stories and read briefly into it.

So during our first session, we "talked" to three different "spirits" and then got Zaza and Mama with the rapid back and forth action as noted in other stories. It said that it liked my boyfriend but not me. It also said it was jealous of me because of the relationship my boyfriend and I have. We closed the session by having it run over GOODBYE on the board. We then burned sage and allowed the smoke to run over the board. At this point, I stated that I was a little concerned. But my boyfriend felt we had nothing to worry about.

About a month or two went by without touching the board, when strange things began to occur. We heard voices, had battery operated items turn on by themselves, saw shadow movement, heard footsteps, felt as if there was something with us, and once my boyfriend thought I had come home, hearing and seeing movement in the kitchen, even though I didn't get home for another half an hour.

Due to all the activity, my boyfriend felt that perhaps the spirits wanted us to talk. So we pulled out the board again. We talked with two other spirits but were interrupted by Zaza and Mama. Again, I felt as if the spirit was negative but he did not agree. Once again we closed the session in the same and burned sage.

It has been about a couple months since we last got it out, and I started to feel as if I was being watched by something negative when I was alone. I told the boyfriend about it but he stated that it was probably in my head or I was nervous because I was alone at night.

We decided to use the board last night and immediately Zaza came on. After spelling its name, it spelled out KILLS followed by letters that did not seem to make sense.

I decided to find out what it wanted and put up a stand. At first it would only answer yes or no questions and would just spell out its name if it was asked to elaborate on something, though it was able to tell the years my parents were born (information my boyfriend doesn't know). It stated that it does not like my boyfriend, doesn't like me, and has been following me for a while. It finally began to spell when asked if it wanted to hurt me. It spelled out YES and then spelled out it wanted to KILL me. It also stated that it didn't like my boyfriend but didn't intend to hurt him. It stated that it was the cause of my constant nightmares and that it would not leave me. It attempted to go through the numbers backwards but stopped when I told it to, and it also tried the same thing with GOODBYE when closing, but also corrected itself when I said to run over the word forwards.

The thing is, I have felt that there has been something with me at various points in my life, and have heard and seen things prior to this. What can I do to stop what is going on because I don't want to have to live with this my entire life.

From her description, Rhonda has had a greater than average sensitivity to the spirit world throughout her life. Thus, she might be a "thin-boundary" person, more easily affected by even a board personality than most other people. Such individuals often discover their vulnerability the hard way, through an unpleasant attachment. They must learn how to improve their barriers. Opportunistic spirits such as the Z-entities will seize an advantage and act out just as Zaza/Mama did in Rhonda's case, creating disturbing phenomena and making dire threats.

In the next case, Zozo appears first, then Zaza and Mama, and when Mama shows up, the entity seems to indicate that it "wants" the unborn children of a young woman who might be pregnant:

My name is Dave... Me and my girlfriend have encountered ZOZO numerous times. We first got the Ouija board back during Christmas time and my girlfriend's dad used to come through, who passed about three years ago. At least that's what the board said. Then all of a sudden the board wouldn't cooperate and would do figure eights and was trying to go to each corner. We decided not to use it anymore. It just stuck on my mind constantly and I finally decided to try it once more. We didn't even get to ask the spirit's name and he just started spelling ZOZOZOZOZOZOZOZO.

At first he acted as if he was good and nice. But then he got mean and said he was going to hurt us and spelt my girlfriend's name out, so we said goodbye and put sea salt on the board. We put it away for six weeks and this past weekend decided to try it out again.

Her father and ZOZO, ZAZA, and MAMA came through. And it [planchette] would move before we would ask questions and it just kept spelling out my girlfriend's name. I finally asked why he [spirit] was so obsessed with her and he spelt BABYS 2 BABYS 2 MAMA WANTS. I asked if he was trying to say she was pregnant and he shot over to YES and shot down to 2. So I asked twins.

He said yes ALICE BABYS 2. We are going to a doctor
today to see if he was right. I think we are done for now.

We were unable to verify whether or not Alice was indeed
pregnant—it is not unusual for experiencers to drop out of sight once
they have shared their primary story. Based on the number of cases we
have in which the Z-entities have given accurate personal information,
we suspect that the pregnancy information was correct.

Sometimes Mama goes from negative to nice, and then, when
users have dropped their guards, zooms back to negative. This next
account has all the warning signs of major trouble:

I have two friends... A few months ago, we were all
depressed, suicidal, and two of us were cutting ourselves.
They were both at my house for break, and I had recently
discovered my house was haunted. I'm very sensitive to
spirits and energies, and I actually saw a man in a brown
coat standing in my living room. My mother suggested we
bring out the Ouija board that we had, which, surprisingly,
none of us had known where it came from. It was just
there one day.

While we were on it, we met some spirits, all
who told us something about "fire," "car," and "rape." My
mother went with my sister to pick up my stepfather, and
told us not to do it [the board] while she wasn't home.
Well, being thirteen, we did. We thought it was fun, we
were making friends.

But the next time we got one, we got MAMA.
She told us she had murdered those children on a car
ride, and when we asked her how old she was she put
in random numbers. She soon became malicious and
started calling us names and threatening to hurt us. This
went on for a while, and the eye would start violently
shifting from M to A, over and over. Eventually she went
away. She would talk to us. But this little girl would tell us
that MAMA wanted to hurt her. She was terrified.

A week later, we did it again. MAMA was very
sweet and loving to us. Tonight, I saw the words MAMA
and ZOZO in a review. I found out about all of this, and

now I'm aching to learn more. Thanks for reading, we're
actually planning to speak with the Ouija again soon.

Vacillations from good to bad to good are intended only to
confuse board users, and lull them into a false sense that everything is
fine. Whenever this pattern emerges, it is definitely time to close the spirit
door. Continuing the connection can lead to more severe problems.

## Lily

Mama has its own alter ego, another feminine name: Lily. Lilies are
symbols of spiritual purity, but this Z-entity is the opposite of pure.
"Lily" in this context is short for Lilith, the dreadful mother of all
demons in lore. She is a demon of the night and a succubus who flies
about searching for newborn children to kidnap or strangle, and
sleeping men to seduce in order to produce more demon children. Lilith
creates nightmares and attacks mothers and their infants—fetuses are
not out of the question, either.

Lilith is a major figure in Jewish demonology, appearing as early
as 700 BCE in the book of Isaiah; she or beings similar to her also are
found in myths from other cultures around the world. She is the dark
aspect of the Mother Goddess. She is the original "scarlet woman" and
sometimes described as a screech owl, blind by day, who sucks the breasts
or navels of young children or the dugs of goats.

In addition to Jewish folklore, Lilith appears in various forms
in Iranian, Babylonian, Sumerian, Canaanite, Persian, Arabic, Teutonic,
Mexican, Greek, English, Asian, and Native American Indian legends.
She is sometimes associated with other characters in legend and myth,
including the Queen of Sheba and Helen of Troy. In medieval Europe,
she was often portrayed as the wife, concubine or grandmother of Satan.

Lilith appears in different guises in various texts. She is best
known as the first wife of Adam, created by God as twins joined in the
back. Lilith demanded equality with Adam, and, failing to get it, left
him in anger. Adam complained to God that his wife had deserted him.
God sent three angels, Sanvi, Sansanvi, and Semangelaf, to bring Lilith
back to Eden. The angels found her in the Red Sea and threatened her
with the loss of one hundred of her demon children every day unless she
returned to Adam. She refused and was punished. Lilith took revenge
by launching a reign of terror against women in childbirth, newborn

infants—particularly males—and men who slept alone. She was forced, however, to swear to the three angels that whenever she saw their names or images on an amulet, she would leave infants and mothers alone.

Lilith is said to produce one hundred demon offspring every day, who are called *lilim*. Her daughters specialize in sorcery, seduction, and strangulation.

As with the other Z-entities, Lily comes along in different combinations, sometimes with Mama, sometimes with Zozo or Zaza. Sometimes Lily appears first and with a sweet or sympathetic demeanor, and then is followed by a meaner Zozo or Zaza. In other cases, it is the reverse. Lily's appearances on the board may be brief, which often confuses users, who assume "Lily" is a human.

In this account, Lily asks for help in order to engage the board users:

> Hello, my name is Nicki. I live in Tulsa, Oklahoma. I went to [store] in about February to buy a glow in the dark Ouija board. Well, last weekend me and my friends decide to play with it. We met this nice spirit named Lily, and she needed help we were trying to help her but nothing worked.
>
> Later that night around witching hour (12 AM), she left. We then again asked if anyone was there. It said ZOZO. We didn't think anything about it. We asked questions and she seemed friendly. So we all got up and went to the living room with the board still out. we sat around talking and drinking soda. After about ten minutes we put our glasses in the sink and went back to her room only to discover that the board was gone! We looked everywhere for it. So after a while we gave up and went back into to the living room to find it there. So we went back into the room and played with it some more.
>
> At about 3:33 AM my pony tail holder broke and my hair went over my face and I guess I blacked out. My friends said I was possessed and that when Lily came back she said ZOZO her sister is in the room. They asked where and the pointer flew to me. They said I tried to hurt them, that I was speaking a different language—Latin they said it was.

The most freaky thing was that we had a candle lit and when ZOZO left I was waking back up. The candle was out and when we turned on the lights, the center of the candle was gone, no wick, nothing. It was like a cup without the bottom. This happened six times though out the night and we used brand new candles every time. But I believe I was possessed by the demon ZOZO.

The next experiencer suffers after-effects following a board session in which Zozo and Lily manifest:

My name is Betty. I am from Tulsa, Oklahoma and have had two very weird experiences with a Ouija board. I borrowed one that belonged to a friend, thinking it was a fun game and was just a joke. I got a small lavender candle and made sure my room was dark. I had done the board with my friend before, and thought she had a trick to it. I did the set up, and asked if there was anyone there.

At first it didn't move, so I thought it was fake. Then the cursor shot out of my hand. I checked my windows and everything but had no explanation. I asked it again, and slowly, it moved to spell ZOZO... then LILY? It had done this before, and since I knew it wasn't fake, was very scared. I had heard stories about her before, and was worried. I asked if it knew anything about me, and it described to me a dream I had had the night before. I was kinda freaked.... especially when she told me the main character was her, Zozo. I immediately put up the board, but still can't help but feel as if I'm being watched?

One night, I had another dream about her and it involved me being killed by one of my friends, who tuned out to be ZoZo??? Weird and unexplainable things have been happening to me, and I feel I may be being haunted by her. I believe in it all, now.... very much. I just wish other people knew about these stories and did, too.

In the next account, Lily masquerades as a little girl:

My name is Danny, I live in Australia. Three years ago towards the end of the year I started getting mixed up in Ouija boards with a few people from my school. My school is about fifty meters in front of an old train station, no trains have run on the tracks for years and nobody ever walked along them, and there was this one little shack that they did the Ouija in. At the start everything was fine, it was fun, and seemingly addictive. We started talking to an entity claiming to be the spirit of a four-year-old girl named Lily, who died in a car crash with her mother.

Lily talked to us every day. She was so polite and she always warned us when demons were around, but just before she'd mention anything, I'd get this feeling in my stomach just telling me something was wrong.

After a few weeks of chatting between Lily, and another spirit named Jack, things started to turn bad, I'd noticed a change in the weather around the same time that we were always surrounded by demons. Most days it wasn't safe for us to walk back to school when lunch ended so we had to wait until the demons left. I only really knew one of the four people that I was doing it with, we were pretty close friends at the time.

Then one night, we both had very vivid, terrifying dreams, and they felt real, as if we were astral projecting. These dreams continued for three nights, and every dream was the same, dark, scary, and I was being followed by demons trying to kill me wherever I went. After the third night I couldn't handle it anymore, so we all went to do another Ouija to find out what was going on. I'm not a dumb kid, and I don't like being left in the dark either, also my OCD [obsessive compulsive disorder] makes me want to know everything in perfect detail.

No spirits wanted to talk to me, they all of a sudden turned on me, they ignored me when I asked questions, so someone had to repeat what I was asking.

They asked what was up with the dreams. Before it even got all the way to the Z, I asked, "Zozo?" and it moved to YES.

After that I freaked and legged it back down to school because I'd already read up all about him and knew it was not good news. The others stayed back and continued talking, and eventually were talking to Zozo, and he let slip that he was going to kill me in two days. I had broken up with my girlfriend the day before, and of course I still had feelings for her, and of course, she absolutely hated me, and I know demons will try and hurt the people you care about to get to you, so she was my only concern at the time, and I didn't want to drag her down with my burden.

Two days later, I got to school, and was shocked to see her running towards me with a worried look on her face. Her mum's girlfriend has visions, and she went to bed that night, and dreamt of me and my friend doing a Ouija and talking to Zozo, and I got flung up to the wall and choked to death and there was nothing there. So I stopped doing Ouijas then.

From then until March 16th this year, I was haunted by demons, I heard their voices saying my name on odd occasions. Some days I couldn't turn a corner without coming face to face with a black figure that disappeared about a second later. I cut all emotional attachments, I lost my friends, I distanced from my family, and worst of all, every day that went by, one thought played on my mind, "either demons are real, and want me dead, or demons aren't real, and I'm crazy." Throughout that time I dreamt of so many things that happened, I even dreamt my dad's death. I started having premonitions, and then I also started getting more gut feelings about things, that would tell me what to do and what not to do. The paranormal took over my life. I know things that no kid at that age should of [known], I only let a few people in on my life, and believe me, my life before Zozo wasn't any better. Which is why he took such a fond liking to me, I'm always surrounded by negative energy.

My past relationship, well, when you can read your partner's thoughts, and all the things she says that you know are lies, doesn't mix too well. Don't get me wrong, I'm not some f'd up kid, I still function with society, I know what aspects of my life I keep to myself. I'm just a kid who stumbled onto something much greater than him.

Anyways, on my birthday, my sister, her friend, and her friend's boyfriend and I all went for a drive to the possum caves on the edge of town. I knew I have a strong connection with Zozo. If I think about Zozo, and speak as if I was speaking to him, he hears what I'm saying, and I got him to come talk to me. All I did was apologize for everything, I was the biggest wanker to demons, they just have an effect on my mood, and I just can't control it sometimes.

This appears to be another case of someone who has heightened psychic sensitivity, and who has difficulty closing the door to spirit once it is opened. Zozo and its alter egos take advantage of such openings.

Masquerading and shapeshifting from one name and pseudo personality to another is a common tactic used by Zozo. Board users should be wary of any name if the communicator exhibits threatening behavior.

# 10

## Levels of Zozo Encounters

Zozo encounters fall into patterns of characteristics that reveal an escalation of the entity's ability to disturb, disrupt, and destroy. Many people report that strange occurrences continue after they have had an encounter with Zozo or with other Z-entities. Some cases are mundane in nature, but some have involved accidents, rape, suicide, sexual assault, and self-mutilation.

Darren divides cases into three levels of Zozo Encounters. Many experiences overlap.

### Level One Zozo Encounters

Level One is what usually happens when someone using a spirit board experiences either a gradual or sudden movement of the planchette back and from Z to O, which Darren labeled the "rainbow effect." Often the planchette will move in figure eight patterns first, which might be a symbolic inverted Z or infinity sigil. Also typical is the planchette moving in tight spirals and circular movements, both clockwise and counter-clockwise.

The planchette may then exhibit an independent nature. The movements may include undecipherable words, or the running though the alphabet and/or numbers forward or backward.

A Level One experience may involve what seems to be communication with a deceased friend or family member, but is probably a masquerade to get users emotionally involved. Initial messages can be pleasant, even funny and amusing. Answers to questions can be helpful and meaningful, and elicit emotional responses from the players. The board users do not realize that this opening is a deception, paving the way for Zozo. Here is one account:

> My friends and I had not been using the Ouija very long, but we were having fun. At first not much happened, and then one night we got a spirit who said its name was Jake, and he had died in the 1700s. Jake seemed friendly. But he didn't last long. Suddenly the pointer started going crazy, running all over the board and doing weird circles. We knew we weren't controlling it.
>
> Then it started seesawing back and forth between the Z and O. We didn't know what was going on. We got freaked and decided to stop.
>
> One of my friends was looking around on the internet and found Zozo, so we think that's who we contacted. The next time we used the board, we asked for Zozo. We were kind of excited about the idea that we had made contact with a demon, but I admit we are scared, too. The pointer started going crazy again, and then did that funny seesaw between the Z and O.
>
> Zozo answered questions and we were amazed at the accuracy—stuff only one or two of us knew the answers to. We did some more sessions with Zozo, I'm not sure how many. So far nothing bad has happened. Is it safe to continue?

Most Level One Zozo encounters end without a war of words, hostility, or warnings of violence. However, once Zozo reveals itself, it is not a good idea to continue communication.

In this next account, the users were taken aback by Zaza and Mama, even laughed, and wondered what it all meant:

> I tried a Ouija board once, over ten years ago, and it worked for my friends and I. We talked to one of my friend's grandfathers and a little girl from my other friend's church that had passed. I was a little creeped out by the experience, and I didn't use the board again until last night. I was certain it would work.
>
> I was with my boyfriend, his sister, and another couple. (At the other couples' house; I even asked if they were sure and told them I would never use a Ouija board in my house.) The three females tried first, and the planchette began to move, but wasn't making very much sense. The other woman and I stopped, and my boyfriend and his sister put their fingers on the planchette. They began to communicate with their recently deceased father (he passed January of this year), or an entity pretending to be him. He spelled out his own name, but when they asked, "Is this Dad?" the answer was NO.
>
> My boyfriend asked, "What are your initials?" and it spelled the correct initials extremely quickly. It also spelled my boyfriend's Polish name many times, and his sister's Polish name twice. Then it spelled some jibberish and MAMA. Then it kept going ZAZAZAZA. We hadn't heard any of these stories and were actually laughing. I even remember asking, "Does Zaza mean anything in Polish?" (They are both fluent, but I am not.)
>
> My boyfriend's sister got home and looked up Zaza and found all these stories about Mama and Zaza. She is terrified. My boyfriend thinks it is very strange, but is not convinced. I'm not sure what to think!
>
> To top it off, their father said multiple times before he died that he was being haunted by a demon.

No matter how harmless the contact seems, it is not wise to continue. Sometimes board participants who are more experienced will recognize the trickster type behavior of the entity, and properly close the session without pressing the issue.

If the Zozo name or alternate name appears, many participants will recognize it and wisely end the session. It is good to close the portal to the spirit world with prayer, forcefully scooting the planchette over the word GOODBYE, and politely dismiss all spirits without respect. If a protective circle has been set for the session, it should be formally closed.

Level One encounters often escalate to Level Two, especially if board participants become mesmerized with the contact. How quickly the experience escalates to Level Two depends on many factors. The demeanor and circumstances of the participants, the location and ambiance of the session, anxiety, emotions, expectation bias, laws of attraction (fear attracts what is feared), and other nuances can dramatically effect what happens next.

## Level Two Zozo Encounters

A Level Two Zozo encounter is more dramatic. Direct contact with the entity is established, recognized, and repeated. The entity may still pretend to be a deceased relative or friend, and is able to give accurate answers to questions. Middle names, nicknames, and dates of birth and death can be revealed. The planchette moves swiftly, with deliberate intent, using abbreviations so that a quicker communication can be delivered. A mocking tone can develop, with a sinister sense of humor and urgency. Threats of death or sexual assault may spring out of nowhere. A heavy presence may become noticeable to anyone in the room. Here is an account involving Zaza and Mama:

> For around a year now I have been very interested in this Zozo phenomenon. I had wanted to use a Ouija board for a while but never got around to it. When one of my buddies did it, I was excited to hear how it went. He described it as a horrible experience. When he told me he got a spirit named Zaza, I got very excited.
> The story he told me matched others' experiences very closely. He had never heard of Zaza until he looked it up after his Ouija session. It kept telling him and the other users to kill each other. It would answer impossible math questions, answer personal questions, and even tell

them who was going to call, and sure enough that person would call minutes later. It apparently would focus on one user especially and would constantly tell him to die.

I decided to attend the next time they used the Ouija board. First time nothing very significant happened, except it kept going to NZ. The next night however it would move very fast between Z and A, also M and A. It would also constantly move in circular motions. I brought a digital camera and would ask it to show itself on the camera. I didn't notice anything in most pictures but in one I can see a smoky-looking skull with eye sockets, a nose, and two long fangs right next to the board in the glass.

Level Two encounters can enter realms of the unexplainable. Objects may move of their own volition. Candle flames may be blown out as though by an invisible breath. Lights may flicker on and off, and doors will lock on their own, or be flung open expectantly. The planchette may fly off of the board with tremendous force.

In many Level Two encounters, a spirit attachment may happen, either suddenly or slowly over a period of time without the participants' realization. Repeated contact becomes necessary, even obsessive, on the part of the board users.

Here is a Level Two case, from a woman:

Since the first time I have touched a Ouija board a demon that calls himself Z has been attached to it. He says he loves me and I am his, and there has even been time he has taken hold of my friends while we are playing. Also recently, my roommate say she hears like something pounding on my walls when no one is there, and I feel like I'm being watched, and I feel my bed move, and my back or arms feel like they are on fire or like someone is grabbing me. It don't really hurt but it bothers me, and he says he won't hurt me and that he is always gonna be nice to me, but after reading your site I don't know if I can trust him. A lot of strange things have been happening.

Zozo is deceptive, and its promises are always broken. The entity is clearly hurting the user, but there seems to be an obsession or compulsion to continue using the board. We always recommend that when these events occur, the users stop their board activity and seek help.

In many Level Two encounters, the entity may decide to take total control of the board. Attempts to make contact with other spirit entities become unsuccessful, with the exception of other Z-entities or the powerful "Mama" entity. A bizarre tug of war for control of the board may happen with multiple entities fighting for control.

In the following account, a woman relates experiences in which she and her friends first think they are talking to the dead, then get Z, Zaza, and Mama. The entities actually argue among themselves as to who they are:

Not this Halloween but the one prior, a friend of mine [and I] played several times [on the board] on that day and a few times after. During our conversations when we would ask who we were speaking to, it would either say Z, or Zaza, or it was Mama. Shortly before we played, my "mema" [grandmother] had passed, so I thought maybe it was her. Then it would pretend to be my dad (who had killed himself years prior). They would fight back and forth whether it be my mema and Z or my father and [name], like there was some power struggle with the board.

We started getting freaked out the last time we played, because we had a cross on the board made of silver and it literally spiraled up off the board. Three people saw. We all started feeling a very angry/heavy feeling in the air. Then we saw a dark cloud in the kitchen hovering. That night we decided to no longer play.

So since then [a year later], a lot of weird things have happened...

--One day I could see a male shape/figure looking in on me through my bathroom door, I turned around, nothing there.

--Another time my daughter saw a figure in her closet.

--Next my daughter saw a black cloud-like object floating over her in the shower.

--One night my daughter was in my bathroom and heard heavy footsteps coming towards the door (despite we had carpet). She woke me up by screaming, "Mom!" and the door of the bathroom that was closed flung open. It really scared her.

Finally, I bought some sage because I heard that worked well. Our house felt fine for a while until one morning I woke up to glass breaking. I had a candle holder that was on top of my fridge (in the back of some appliances) that was holding the sage in one of the holders. The entire thing somehow flew over the appliances and shattered all over my kitchen floor. This piece probably weighed a good three to five pounds. The sage was also on the floor in the broken glass.

We also have had glasses fly off the counter and break and generally a heavy feeling present majority of the time.

Since then we have moved. Then last night we were watching a movie (me, my other daughter and two other people), and out of nowhere our star on the top of our Christmas tree flew off the tree towards us. My daughter still feels like something is here, though she was with friends last night and always feels like something is watching her. I don't know if any of this has to do with Z but if so I was wondering if you had any suggestions on how to get rid of it. We have also since returned the board to the people who we were borrowing it from and they gave it to someone else.

A common tell-tale sign of a Level Two encounter is a noticeable change in the atmosphere, sounds that emanate from thin air such as breathing, whispers, maniacal laughing, and banging or thuds from within walls. Any number of strange phenomena may occur—the entity uses these to instill fear and anxiety. The more fear it can bring forth, the better and more dramatic the manifestation of phenomena. One may experience the heavy sensation of being watched, even after board usage.

With repeated contact, the entity employs a cunning and deceptive game of cat and mouse. It may decide to attack the "weakest link" in the home, such as a child, teenager, or non-participant. In almost all Level Two encounters, the entity shows calculated anger, even rage, as well as jealousy and a distinctive preponderance for death threats. Hundreds of cases report the entity will express sexual desire for specific participants. Often it will embarrass females by announcing their menstrual cycles, or someone on whom they have a secret crush. This seeming ability to read minds of participants increases feelings of panic and helplessness.

## Level Three Zozo Encounters

Level Three encounters are rarer, as most people will recognize the potential dangers that are developing, and will end the sessions and avoid the board. Some people just cannot get enough, however, and get caught up in the thrill of danger. They become at risk for attachment and even stages of possession. They experience mental oppression: dark thoughts that do not seem to be their own, often urging them to violence or suicide. Victims may have repeated thoughts of criminal violence, or to cause bodily harm to friends or loved ones. Their behavior changes in noticeable ways. They become withdrawn, depressed, or angry, or do irrational things. They may have sudden psychic powers, such as knowledge of hidden or lost objects, or information they have no way of knowing naturally. Hallucinations can occur.

The entity can now override spirit board communication and exchange words and thoughts via telepathy. The victim may have frequent vivid nightmares and sleep deprivation, leading to a deterioration of health. They may suffer accidents, bad luck, and problems coping with work and domestic relationships.

The following story illustrates how deterioration can happen:

> Hello. My name is Douglas. I believe I have been in contact with Zozo. It all started when my friend Molly was being haunted by "Bloody Mary" and was having dreams and waking up with unexplained scratches. I went to her house to play Ouija. We contacted Zozo, and Zaza. They referred to themselves as Zoaz (a combo of Zozo and Zaza). They said that they had always been with her and loved her very much.

Later on in September of 2014, me and my friends played at my birthday party. Zozo came back. He said he loved me and that he wanted to protect me and make me not be sad. (I was diagnosed with depression and anxiety in 2012 and have been living with it since). He became connected to my other friends, Karen, Annie, and Chris.

Then Mama started talking to us. Zozo said she wanted to hurt us and that she was very angry with him and us. Karen and Annie dropped out because they were scared and didn't want any more to do with the board.

Fast forward to currently, me and Chris have been playing often. The board has been going in a rainbow-like motion to Z-O-Z-O-Z-O over and over. It said that if I did that twenty times it could come out of the board. We let it do that. I proceeded to get scared and asked Zozo to leave and go back into the board. He then apologized and said he loved me very much and would never hurt me.

However, since I met Zozo I have made two trips to the hospital for suicide attempts. I've been doing a lot of research that says he latches on to people with depression, and makes it worse. I'm looking for any information you may be able to give me, and an explanation as to why he hasn't done anything like knock on walls, make noises, or appear. Is it because he "loves me"?

Zozo does not love anyone—that is a deception designed to fool people and encourage them to be vulnerable. These board players made a serious mistake in giving the entity permission to leave the board if it performed according to their request. Even though Zozo supposedly returned to the board, it now has a way out at any time.

Not all phenomena we describe happen in every single encounter, even though the dominant patterns may be present.

Individuals who have health issues, especially depression, emotional trauma and upset, and mental conditions, may more vulnerable than others to spirit attachments. In such cases, individuals should avoid spirit contact activities of all kinds.

The insidious nature of Zozo encounters of all levels leads many victims to conclude that Zozo is demonic. There are other possible explanations as well, as we discuss in the next chapter. We have discovered that Zozo's tracks go way back in human history. It seems this entity has had many dark encounters with human beings.

## A three-level experience with Z

The following story describes an escalation of unpleasant phenomena after a spirit board was used in a haunted, contaminated environment. When the energy of place is bad, it can influence the nature of any kind of spirit communication:

> I'm going to start from the beginning. I didn't make the connection of how significant Z was in the experiences I've had till today when I stumbled across an article with several people sharing their experiences with him. When I was six, my mom and stepdad bought their first home, an old but yet beautiful large fixer upper. At first things seemed okay. Then I started to notice things. More like weird feelings at first. Just an overwhelming uneasy feeling when I was alone at times.
>
> Then one day a neighbor girl and I were sitting on my sofa while my mom and step dad were unpacking. I was sitting by a box of VHS tapes and pulled one out that looked really scary and pretended to read it to the girl, making up the scariest story possible. Then suddenly I felt a stinging sensation on my leg. When I looked down I had a very large scratch that was bleeding. There was nothing there that could have scratched me. We had been sitting there for quite some time staying out of the way. My mom didn't believe me and blamed our black lab, Bear, even though he was outside at the time.
>
> One day while playing in our dining room, I looked up and for a brief second saw a little girl peeking at me through the spindles on our stairs. When I glanced back she was gone. I told my mom, but yet again I was "seeing things."

A few weeks later I was outside playing with a different neighbor girl and she asked me if I had seen the little girl that sits on my stairs. I dragged her in my house to tell my mom because I was so upset she didn't believe me. My mom asked her mom if she had ever told her stories of seeing a little girl in our house and she said that the people that lived in our house right before us dabbled in black magic and sacrificed stray cats in our dining room, trying to bring forth a demon. She said she had been in our house and seen the chandelier spin in circles in our dining room. My mom was really freaked out considering the rug she had thrown out that was left in our dining room had dark brown stains all over it.

Then one night the dreams started. I dreamt that I was walking through our house through the living room by our stairs. I saw a pregnant lady standing by a really pretty stained glass window on the middle landing of our stairs, crying with her head down holding her belly. She turned to look at me and I woke up. I told my mom in the morning while getting ready for school. Thought it was weird, but the window on our stairs was plain old regular glass. Nothing like the colorful window in my dream.

I didn't think much of it till a few weeks later when my mom started questioning me about the dream, when she hadn't cared before. She had tea earlier that day with our elderly neighbor while I was at school. She told mom some history about our house. A dentist and his family had built the house, and while there they had lost two children to pneumonia, a baby and a little girl. The lady then told her she took care of the mother when she was an old woman and that she was a drunk. When the woman died, the crazy demon lady bought the house, and then lost it in foreclosure. Then we unluckily moved in. She went on to say it was a shame the woman that owned it before us stripped the house of the stained glass window that was on the landing of our stairs. My mom kept asking me how I knew, and all I could say was I saw it in my dream.

A couple months went by and my parents start to fix up the house, which seems to stir up all sorts of new things. First a black shadow, shapeshifting thing that would shoot past you or you would catch out the corner of your eye. But this time my mom would see it, too.

Then one day I was being kinda bad and got sent to my room. So me and my dog go in and head upstairs to my room. It is broad day light and I don't have a fear in the world. I go in my room for two minutes, get antsy and decide to go down the hall to the bathroom. As I walk past the steps I hear heavy footsteps coming up the stairs toward me, but see no one. I think it's my stepdad, but when the footsteps hit the landing and I should see someone, there's no one there. But the stomping, angry sounding footsteps are still coming towards me! My dog starts to growl and show his teeth. Then the fear that paralyzed me left long enough for me to run with my dog in tow and hide in the bathroom with my eyes covered till my mom came to get me.

Sometime later my mom had the same experience while she was home alone getting ready for work. She was upstairs in the bathroom and thought my stepdad came home early because she heard the same loud steps. But came to find no one was there at all. The black shadow was seen all the time along with a tall shadow man in the basement.

Once we were having our house rewired and there were guys all through our house cutting small holes to put in new circuit outlets. I went to the restroom and would look through the circuit hole into one of our bedrooms just to make sure I didn't have an audience. But when I looked through the room was different. Nicer it looked, new. A woman with blonde hair was rocking with her back to me in a white wooden rocking chair. She was humming a song. I felt comfortable, not scared. Then she sensed that I was there and started to turn to look at me. She was holding a baby, smiling. But her smile was evil and sent chills through me. This was the lady I dreamt about when we first moved in. I jumped back, fell, and hit my head on the toilet.

One day I was lying on the couch watching a movie while my mom was upstairs taking a bath. She yelled for me and when I got up there was a bunch of white lights in the shape of a very tall man. He was blocking my route to the steps. Our downstairs was a giant circle of four rooms and we had sliding wooden doors to separate them. I ran the other way and hit the steps with a speed I didn't know was possible for me. I made it to my mom in seconds to hear she had seen it to. Not in a set form. But a blob of floating white lights that hovered by her in the tub. We figured white lights had to be good and dismissed it as a loved one.

Then one night I had a friend over and we were playing with one of those girl talk voice recorders. We had watched a show about ghosts and messages coming through on tape recorders. She was one of the few friends that would stay in my house. No one else would ever come back after a night there. We decide to ask a few questions. When we play it back there's nothing on the tape. Then we figured we would leave it on when we went to sleep.

The next morning, we get up and the first thing we do is play back the tape. About twenty minutes in, we hear a baby crying, then glass breaks. Then sudden silence for a second. Then a dog starts barking and a woman begins screaming, then it all comes to an abrupt stop, and there's nothing else on the tape. We played it for my mom and she thought we accidently recorded a movie, even though my TV was off.

My stepdad went years before seeing anything, but once had a weird dream at the same time as my mom about an invisible force attacking us. Us kids were outside, and the force was not letting my mom out the house. His dream was him not able to get free. They awoke totally freaked out.

My stepdad had nightmares every day for most of his life, but he thought nothing of it till one day when I was gone to my dad's for the night. He got to see what happened to us every time he worked night-turn. Lights, radios, and TVs turning on and off, the volume going up and down, doors opening and closing, and the sound of like dressers being knocked over and thrown around upstairs. He was scared and walked around with a bat, thinking someone had broken in. My mom laughed at him because in some sick way we were used to it. Me and her had experiences every day that made him think we were crazy. For years we all slept in the living room together. It was a four-bedroom house. As I got older, I wanted privacy, and my mom and stepdad fixed my room up real nice, and I was the only one to sleep upstairs. Everything was calm for a long time.

Then for my 13th birthday, I went shopping with my mom for games for my sleep-over and came across a Ouija board. My friends and I asked stupid girly questions. But the next day my mom wanted to play with it to make contact with the ghosts in our house, to learn more about them, and maybe have some peace.

At first it claimed to be a little girl. Then Z. He would answer questions for us, but hated my stepdad. My stepdad said he knew a witch while growing up, and he was very against Ouija boards because they open a door to evil. I thought he was crazy. But when we would sneak and play, Z would say my stepdad's coming and we would hide the board. Sure enough, he would burst into my room knowing what we were doing, but didn't catch us.

My mom became obsessed, but the board wouldn't work for her without me. She would wake me up in the middle of the night and beg me just to put my finger on it for a few questions. Its force and presence became stronger, especially in my room. I always slept with my door locked. It was the only way I felt safe— which doesn't make sense to me now because I was locking myself in with it.

My mom would beat on my door and tell me to turn my TV down or off, and same with my radio. I would sleep sound through it. Lights turning off and on. It was weird—I was only a sound sleeper in that house. My step dad wanted it [Z] gone and said we had to close the portal we opened in my room. He put candles on four corners and asked who he was talking to. It hesitated...

then said Z. He told him he needed to leave, that is was his house. It [the pointer] went to NO fast. Then my step dad screamed, "Leave!" and one of the candles by me exploded. All the glass went towards my stepdad. I jumped up and was so scared.

After that things calmed down slightly. Still a lot of activity, but it seemed harmless. At that time, I truly believed the little girl that passed away there was somehow trapped in my house with whatever evil spirit Z was. I felt some weird connection to her and wanted to help her.

One night I had just got a new water bed and we filled it. It was so cold I decided to sleep on a twin mattress on the floor till my bed warmed up. Through the night I was a little restless and went to roll over in my sleep, but glanced around me as I rolled over. I saw glimpse of a little girl standing at the foot of my mattress. I think it's my baby sister and start talking to her but stay rolled over. I say, "Cynnie, my bed is too small tonight, but I promise you can sleep with me tomorrow." When she doesn't answer me, I realize, wait, my doors are locked. I never got up and let her in. I turn over and it isn't my sister. It's a little girl with long dark hair similar to hers, in a long white night gown. But her eyes are big black holes. I jump up and she disappears, but as she does my light, TV, and radio all turn on. I'm fourteen years old and terrified like a little baby. I ran downstairs and slept with my mom and brother and sister in the living room.

Some time goes by, and I'm at my dad's house for the night. I get ready for bed and laid down. I can't fall to sleep and want to turn the TV on, but can't because I have school in the morning and my dad will hear it. I toss and turn and look at the clock. Then it gets cold and I snuggle into the blanket. But I notice a green light coming from the windows that flows into the room quickly. Then I feel a sudden heaviness on my chest like I'm pinned. I can't breathe. I can't scream. I think I'm going to die. Then I think, *f-- this*, and fight with everything in me to sit up then stand up. My body feels so heavy and I want to scream for help but it won't come out. I get to the door, which was literally two feet away, but it was so hard to reach. I grab the door knob turn and pull. Once it comes open the force lets go. I scream and fall to the kitchen floor. My dad runs to me, scared, but once I tell him what happened, he says it was a dream, but agrees to let me stay in his room.

The next morning on my way to school he tells me I was talking in my sleep about demons and asked what I was dreaming about, but I didn't remember like I normally do. When I came home from school I told my mom what happened. She looked upset and proceeded to tell me that she had never thrown the board out when my stepdad closed the portal. She had still been playing it. She was playing it when something attacked me at my dad's house. I felt unsafe and terrified. I never thought what was in my house could leave my house. My mom threw the board out and things calmed down, other than the little creepy feelings like someone's behind you, along with the urge to run down the stairs.

My mom and step dad split up for some time. My mother, brother, sister, and I moved in with my grandma. My stepdad lost our house in foreclosure and moved with his sister. Things were good. But I had nightmares almost every night, always somewhat the same. I still live there and I'm scared of a force I can't see walking through the house, waiting for it to get me. Or, I'd see a man that was all skin hunched down to the ground that would run at me like a dog/monkey that sounded like hooves hitting the floor.

I once dreamed my stepdad was going to fight this force and went up the stairs towards it and I chased after him. But by the time I hit the landing he was gone into the darkness of our upstairs and I stopped, scared, hearing it breathe. I can't see it, but it hits me and spins around me and shoots out of me. I'm paralyzed, can't move, can't yell for help. Then I wake up. I dreamt this for years, sometimes I'd force myself up the stairs before it attacks me. Sometimes I get to my room, and so on.

My mom and step dad get back together and we all move to a new house. I try to forget about our old house, but every night the dreams remind me. Then in June 2007, I graduated high school. I'm at a party with a friend and a small group of her friends. We had all had a few beers but weren't drunk. Someone started telling ghost stories. My friend volunteers me to tell some of mine. Everyone was really interested, especially when I said my old house was a couple doors up and abandoned. We all decided to go up on the outdoor porch and look in a big picture window, when some cocky guy who thought I was full of crap about what had happened to me figured out the door to the screened in porch was unlocked. Everyone walked in while he held the door open. I was the last to go in, then that guy behind me. He started to freak out and said the door was pushing him in. I thought he was joking until he physically pushed the door hard with force, jumped the porch, and ran. Compared to the eighty-degree weather outside the porch was freezing cold. The window by the giant wood door was broke out and my friend stuck her hand in to unlock the door. I was scared to death and didn't want to go. Every hair on my body was standing up. She pulls her hand out and has a skeleton key in her hand. I had never seen a skeleton key before in our house. She hands it to me and I unlock the door. We walk in and the stairs going upstairs are covered in ice! It's summer! We do a walk-through of the whole house and get creeped out and leave.

We all jump off the porch and run around the house through the field. There's one girl behind me and one in front. It feels like something jumps on my back and my legs buckle. But I don't fall, I fight it, and as soon as I hit the street, the weight lifts and I can run easily now. We get back to the house and the girl that was behind me says she saw something come at me from under the porch. She said it started as a shadow and then looked like an all-skin guy running like a dog. I went home and went to bed.

The next morning, I awoke to my stepdad coming home from work in Indiana three days early. He says to me, "I know what you did." I'm stunned, thinking someone saw me. He then says he had a dream last night that I went in that house. He asked why I would do that. Why I would go back around it. That I really messed up now.

My step dad was killed in a freak accident a few weeks later, on July 5. After that I swore not to think any more about Z, the little girl spirit, or ever to touch a Ouija board again. A few months later, I got a call that the house burned down. I was kinda sad, I had so many memories there.

I hoped with the house gone, the nightmares would stop, but they didn't. In 2010 I rolled over in bed and saw this skinned-type man-thing hunched down, watching me and my boyfriend and our two young children sleep. I freaked and starting screaming, woke everyone up and it was gone. I told my boyfriend for the first time about everything, and he said he had once dreamed about something like that, but hadn't remembered his dreams in a long time.

We moved soon after, and found out we were expecting another baby. One night my oldest daughter said she didn't like our new house because a guy with bloody hands walks in and out of our room into hers at night. I had the house blessed and the lady told me I had something clinging to me but didn't want to push any further with repelling it until I gave birth. We moved again to a larger house shortly after our daughter was born. And I lost contact with her, kinda thinking she was wrong.

Now at our new house we both have seen shadows out the corner of our eyes. My oldest started having nightmares about a grandma-like lady with black eyes that scares her. Her exact words. I blessed her room myself and said a prayer with a crystal and asked God to clear any evil from around my children. No more nightmares for her since. But mine are still every night almost.

I dreamt once that I was standing in the street in front of my house, in front of hundreds of those skin-looking things, and then I said, smiling, "Aww, come to mama." As they came close, I started killing them with my bare hands. It was very gruesome. And really freaked me out.

I had twins on July 28, 2014. After their birth I didn't remember a single dream up until about a month ago [February 2015]. The dreams have come back and I just want to find a way to move on. He only called himself Z to me. But online when I saw his other name, Zozo, it freaked me out because I have Jimmy Page's symbol from Led Zeppelin, Zoso, tattooed on my wrist. It's just a little too close for my comfort.

I know I told you too much information. But I'm questioning a lot about my past experiences. I don't think there was ever a little girl spirit in my house—I think it was pretending to be something I'd be comfortable with, something I would be sympathetic towards. If she was good, why the black holes for eyes? My daughter dreamed of an elderly woman that made her feel safe like a grandma would, but had big black eyes that scared her. Maybe he [Z] was in my house before the Ouija board, because of the lady that tried to bring in demons by sacrificing cats. I don't know. But I do know I've tried to forget and my dreams don't let me. The lady telling me something is clinging to me has me worried. Especially now that it has affected my daughter. You know more about whatever Z is. What do you think? Please help me. The nightmares continue to this day. I sometimes still feel his presence all though the last time I saw him in person was in 2010. I know I sound crazy. But I need to better understand and rid him from my life.

Clearly, the house itself held negative energy and presences, a good environment for Zozo to manifest once the spirit board was introduced. Was the entity already present, and just assumed its "board identity" once the board was used? Or was it drawn in? Many situations like this provide no clearly defined circumstances.

Our recommendations for remedial steps, as well as preventative measures, for Zozo cases are given later on in this book.

# 11

## Who is Zozo?

Zozo and his alter egos exhibit all the traits of a trickster spirit or even a demon—but do we really know who—or what—Zozo is? Throughout our research, we looked for a "common dark thread" that could connect the different aspects of the phenomenon throughout history, and also the modern outbreak of Zozo encounters on spirit boards. We found many threads, woven together in mysterious ways.

"Zozo is very manipulative," said John Zaffis. "There is a good intelligence base to it. Zozo can seem like a child spirit, deceased relative, or loved one. It has ties to multiple types of things, negative energy, even ancient deities."

Indeed, there are a number of explanations to consider, including one favored by skeptics that has nothing to do with the paranormal. Ultimately, no one explanation may account for Zozo—there may be a variety of explanations, all working in various combinations in any given encounter.

## The ideomotor effect

The simplest explanation for Zozo is one applied to all spirit board activities, and is always cited by skeptics: the ideomotor effect. According to this scenario, Zozo is not a real entity, but is manufactured out of the subconscious. Board users may subconsciously expect or desire "Zozo" to be spelled out, which then causes an involuntary, and often unconscious, response that seems real. In other words, people push the planchette around themselves to fulfill an expectation or desire.

The ideomotor effect theory was introduced in 1852 by William Benjamin Carpenter, a British physiologist. Harvard physician William James wrote about it in his 1890 book, *Principles of Psychology*. The ideomotor effect has been used by debunkers against all forms of facilitated communication, including dowsing, automatic writing, and automatic painting, as well as spirit boards. Even the alternate Z names for Zozo could be summoned up by unconscious impulse.

What exactly happens in the ideomotor effect? Supposedly subconscious thoughts cause minute impulse movements in the muscles to guide the pointer over the letters in some pre-determined manner, even if fingertips are only lightly touching the planchette.

The ideomotor effect cannot be ruled out, of course, and undoubtedly is a factor in some cases where people get the responses they secretly want. However, it cannot account for all movements of the planchette. Sometimes the planchette races around so quickly that the players have a hard time keeping their fingers on it. There also are many cases where the planchette flies off the board, seemingly on its own momentum.

The ideomotor effect also cannot adequately explain all information exchanges, especially lengthy conversations and startling revelations of unknown facts, names, dates, locations of lost objects, and accurate predictions of future events. Darren notes that in many of his own sessions, words would be misspelled in strange ways that he would never do under ordinary circumstances. He also saw strange abbreviations, odd slang terms, and irregular sentence and word combinations that neither he nor his board partner would ever use.

Furthermore, how can the ideomotor effect explain the spelling out of words and sentences, and even slang terms in a foreign language unknown to the players, such as Latin?

There are even more difficulties with the ideomotor explanation. In a situation where several participants are placing their fingers on a planchette, do they all push the planchette around unknowingly, or does one person somehow take control?

Darren witnessed Ouija sessions in which long, drawn out conversations moved with such speed that the players quickly lost the train of thought. An outside observer had to write down the messages just to keep track of the exchange. How does the planchette keep moving when the players start to lose track?

Skeptics counter by claiming that spirit board communications will fall apart if the participants are blindfolded. If the spirits are truly moving the planchette, the people involved should not need to see the board, they argue. In some experiments, blindfolded boards users have difficulty, and in other cases they do not.

In 2014, Darren interviewed a team of researchers at the University of British Columbia who were using Ouija boards to probe the human subconscious. One particular test posed the same factual yes-or-no questions to participants using the board and answering verbally on their own. The subjects were blindfolded when using the board. One partner (not blindfolded) removed their hands from the planchette. The blindfolded subject moved the planchette alone, answering questions, but felt that they were exerting no force on it at all. The subjects answered more questions correctly using the board than when they answered the same questions verbally.

The researchers pointed out that they did not believe these experiments were proof of the paranormal. Nonetheless, the results are intriguing, and demonstrate that perhaps we cannot just dismiss all spirit board communications as generated by the subconscious.

In her book *The Spirits of Ouija*, Karen A. Dahlman describes a board session in which she was blindfolded, and then worked the pointer to spell out a long message involving personal information not known to her—a message from a young deceased woman to her twin sister, who was present at the session.

The ideomotor effect also does not adequately explain the Z names that surface during some sessions—such as Zaza, Zam,

Zagon, and Zepot—that are not known to the players. At first, they are mystified, and then later learn about Zozo and its alter egos.

The following account comes from a doctor who never believed in so-called spirits:

> I am thirty years old, I am a doctor. I never really believed in the Ouija, I was a skeptic, being a man of science. Recently, my little sister (22) brought one over to use, for a night of "scary fun."
>
> The first time the planchette moved, an individual who recently killed themselves contacted us. It turned out to be a friend of someone in the room who was not touching the planchette, to give her a message. After that we were all a bit spooked. The two who were touching the planchette had no idea who this was, or that they ever even existed, for that matter. Only one person in the room did.
>
> Now after that... ZAZA over and over again, spelled out S-E-X, then gibberish. We put the board away. Last night one more time we tried, the planchette spelled out MAMA, at an alarmingly fast pace, as if the planchette was being pushed by myself and another. Upon asking questions of what that means and is it a name? The planchette continued on in a figure eight all around the board (the pictures) and continued on a figure eight all over the board. Even at one point counting down the alphabet backwards from Z to A. When we took our hands off of the planchette it continued to move for another second max on its own.
>
> I just did some research online, and came across your [Darren's] website. I have never heard of Zaza or Mama until now and I'm a bit confused. I am realizing this may be an evil entity trying to harm us. Is this true? Please tell me what to do.

## Super-psi

Debunkers have yet another theory, one that falls back on an old hypothesis advanced in parapsychology in the 1950s, called "super-

ESP." It is now called "super-psi." According to this hypothesis, nonlocal consciousness has the ability to access information anywhere, including the collective. Thus, a medium or even a spirit board user might unconsciously access a psi database without realizing it, and "pull" something from it. Though super-psi cannot be completely ruled out—no one know the limits of consciousness— it is an awkward hypothesis, and cannot explain all kinds of psi, including "drop-in communicators" who show up unannounced at séances. If we were to accept super-psi, we would have to throw out all the entity contact experiences reported throughout the whole of human history.

However, we cannot rule out the possibility of telepathy among participants. If one person anticipates Zozo to appear, could that person affect the thoughts and unconscious motor movements of the others? It may be possible, but how likely is it? Many of the users who encounter Zozo for the first time are not aware of its peculiar patterns of behavior on the board, or that it likes such messages as KILL and MINE.

## Thoughtforms and tulpas

In 2009, an internet meme called Slenderman was created. Slenderman was described as an unusually thin man wearing a black suit, and with a featureless face. Slenderman was said to stalk and abduct people, especially children. Slenderman went viral and took on a life of its own. Increasing numbers of people believed it to be a real supernatural entity, and began reporting encounters.

Slenderman is one of the latest fictional paranormal creations to take on a reality of its own. Around the turn of the twentieth century, competing newspapers battled for readers, and published sensational and lurid stories of mysterious creatures and monsters. One of them was the Snallygaster in Maryland. Soon reports of encounters with the Snallygaster were rampant throughout the mid-Atlantic; people actually believed the monster to be real. Even after the Snallygaster was exposed as a hoax, sightings in multiple states went on for decades, and even today, some people still believe the creature to be real.

Is Zozo a thoughtform created by mass consciousness? Ouija historian Robert Murch notes that Zozo became an internet phenomenon after Darren started his blog and then talked about Zozo on radio shows. "When he started talking about Zozo, it really spread," Murch said.

There are references to Zozo that predate the internet, and we have collected stories from people who encountered Zozo by name long before Darren went public with his blog. Nonetheless, social media undoubtedly has contributed to a collective thoughtform that is accessed unconsciously by board users all over the world. Such a scenario is not out of the question, but whether or not it can explain all Zozo encounters is another matter.

There are interesting aspects of thoughtforms to consider.

## Thoughtforms in magic

In magic, thoughtforms are created on the astral plane and are made up of astral matter, which is a malleable, plastic-like substance that responds to thought. Thoughtforms require intense concentration, otherwise they do not last. Anything can be created as a thoughtform: gods, angels, demons, places, goals, and even activities. Thoughtforms may arise spontaneously out of the collective unconscious as archetypes which take on phantom or seemingly real form. This may explain reports of the Devil, supernatural monsters, entities, nonphysical beings, and otherworldly beings.

Artificial elementals are created by ritual to perform low-level tasks and errands, and to be directed at individuals, to protect or heal, or to harm. To have an effect, thoughtforms must be able to latch on to similar vibrations in the aura of the recipient. If they are unable to do so, they boomerang back to the sender. Thus, one who directs evil thoughts toward another runs the risk of having them return.

The duration of a thoughtform, its strength, and the distance it can travel, depend on the strength and clarity of the original thought. Thoughtforms are said to have the capability to assume their own energy and appear to be intelligent and independent. Equally intense thought can disperse them, or, they can simply disintegrate when their purpose is finished. Some may last years. In magical practice, it is customary to charge a thoughtform with a finite life span, at the end of which it will be reabsorbed back into astral matter.

Thoughtforms radiate out and attract sympathetic essences, thus forming the basis of the law of attraction, which holds that a person manifests on the physical plane what he thinks on *the mental plane.*

Thoughtforms that are not dispersed, as well as some particularly powerful thoughtforms, can go out of control. They wander about looking for energy sources, attaching themselves to people like vampiric entities. Or, they can turn on their creators.

Alexandra David-Neel (1868-1969) was an unusual French woman who created a thoughtform that turned on her. David-Neel had no interest in settling for the life of a homemaker—she wanted to explore far reaches of the world, especially Asia. She was the first woman to enter Llasa, the forbidden capital of Tibet.

David-Neel learned a great deal of Tibetan magic, including how to create a thoughtform called a *tulpa.* Of temporary duration, *tulpas* usually assume human shape and are created to be sent out on a mission. David-Neel sought to create a lama who would be "short and fat, of an innocent and jolly type," as she described it in her autobiography, *Magic and Mystery* in Tibet. After several months of performing the prescribed ritual, a phantom monk manifested. It assumed a life-like form over a period of time, and existed almost like a guest in David-Neel's apartment. The *tulpa* tagged along with her as she went out on a tour.

Then, to her distress, the *tulpa* began to change. She wrote, "The features... gradually underwent a change. The fat, chubby-cheeked fellow grew leaner, his face assumed a vaguely mocking, sly, malignant look. He became more troublesome and bold. In brief, he escaped my control." The *tulpa* began touching her and rubbing up against her in a sexual way. Others began to see him, but he did not respond to anyone's conversation, only to David-Neel.

David-Neel decided to dissolve the *tulpa* in accordance with Tibetan rituals, but the phantom resisted her efforts. It took her six months to eliminate him. The entire episode upset her, and she termed it "very bad luck."

Zozo could fit the pattern of behavior of David-Neel's *tulpa*: funny and amusing at first, then bolder and meaner with audacious sexual moves, then independent strength to resist banishment.

## Thoughtforms in research

Scientific experiments to create thoughtforms have been undertaken, and with success. In the 1970s, a group of parapsychologists under the direction of A.R.G. Owen and his wife, Iris, conducted a series of famous experiments to create a collective thoughtform named "Philip," a discarnate human personality with an artificial life history and background story. The thoughtform was created by group meditation, visualization, and attempts to communicate with it in seances. Several months of no success went by, and then "Philip" took form and began responding to questions via table-tilting and rapping. Sessions with Philip continued for several years, and the group even believed that they succeeded in getting whispery voice responses to questions via Electronic Voice Phenomena on tape. The group wanted to see if Philip would take on an independent personality and give information that had not been created as part of his back story. As lively as the thoughtform became, however, it never went beyond the script.

These examples all demonstrate the power of a thoughtform entity, something created and energized by human beings. The greater the participation, the more energized and active the thoughtform becomes.

If Zozo is a thoughtform, we can certainly see parallels between Zozo's behavior and the traits described in the examples above:

- Zozo acquires enough energy to take on a life of its own and spreads itself around
- Others believe it to be real
- Its behavior goes from pleasant to ugly, and often with sexual overtones
- It is attracted to people who resonate with its own energies (fear, anxieties, thrills)
- It does not go beyond a certain range of behavior or characteristics

As noted above, thoughtforms require an intense amount of concentration and energization in order to exist, and even when some independence is achieved, that energy still must be provided.

Could the world-wide community of spirit board users form a sufficient group mind, or egregor, with that focus? Potentially, yes— but how would this thoughtform have been started, and by whom? Could a Zozo thoughtform rise up and form spontaneously out of the chaos of negative human emotion and thoughts?

When Darren first went public with his personal story on the internet, he was astonished to find others reporting similar experiences, and with the same Zozo name and variations. At that point, there was little, if any, collective awareness of "Zozo." Thus, it appears that Zozo was already in existence and in action. It is likely, however, that the attention generated on the internet has had a viral effect and contributes to a thoughtform projection from people that further energizes Zozo. As Murch mentioned, Darren gave Zozo momentum, and the phenomenon became a snowballing effect with a variety of other contributing factors. Collective interest, discussion, and even shared fear might be sufficient to keep Zozo's engines running for a long period of time. So, if enough spirit board users know about Zozo and fear it, secretly desire to contact it, or openly invite it, they may send out a sympathetic vibration of energy that can help Zozo to manifest.

## Ancient gods and spirits

John Zaffis has suggested that perhaps Zozo was once an ancient deity or god-like spirit who tumbled into the ranks of demons. As Christianity took over the pagan world, the pagan deities and spirits, including demons, were corrupted and relegated to the dark side. Angels, however, evolved to become human allies, except for the fallen ones, who became demons.

For example, the demon Astaroth was formerly a Phoenician fertility goddess, Astarte or Ashtoreth. Asmodeus, another heavy hitter in the Christian pantheon of demons, originally was Aeshma, one of the good, angel-like *amaraspands* of Zoroastrianism. Also, the "spirits" of the celestial realms were turned into demons.

Are there god or demonic candidates for Zozo?

Of interest is The Myth of Zu (also The Epic of Anzu) from Sumerian lore. Zu (full name Anzu) is a monstrous bird of prey who lives in high mountains and preys upon oxen. By flapping its wings, it causes whirlwinds and sandstorms. It is said to have a strange countenance and a roaring voice.

Zu plots to steal the Tablet of Destinies from the chief god, Enlil, in order to gain great, cosmic powers that would enable him to control the world and all the gods, thus disrupting order:

"I shall take the gods' Tablet of Destinies for myself,
And control the orders for all other gods,
And shall possess the throne and be master of the rites!"

While Enlil is bathing in holy water, Zu steals the tablet. The gods panic and search for a hero who will confront Zu and restore the Tablet and order. Ninurta, Enlil's son, takes up the challenge and slays Zu.

The curious association with Zozo is Zu's lust for power. Zozo boasts that it is "the king of kings." Zu attempted to become the ruler of all gods. Zu is also deceitful and cunning, traits shared with Zozo.

## Demons

Most people who encounter Zozo assume the entity to be a demon because of its trickster-to-malicious behavior. In our culture, most people automatically assume demons are all-evil beings working under the direction of Satan. Demons actually fall into a much broader category. A demon is a type of spirit that interferes in the affairs of people. The nature of that interference can vary significantly. The term "demon" actually means "replete with wisdom" and is derived from the Greek term *daimon*. The Greek *daimones* were both good and evil, and even included the ranks of deified heroes. In most cultures, however, demons are troublesome rather than helpful, and many are evil in their actions. They can cause unpleasant hauntings, often involving infestation, oppression, and possession.

Since ancient times, demons have been blamed for all of humankind's problems, such as disease, misfortune, poor health, bad luck, ruined relationships, sin, and soul loss. They can pester humans in sexual ways.

According to magic, demons can be summoned and controlled, and can be tasked.

Zozo exhibits demonic characteristics: tricky, smart, pestering, damaging, sexually precocious, and capable of causing stages of oppression and possession.

In many demonic cases that involve communication, the entity starts out in a familiar pattern we have already discussed: friendly, chatty, wise, and accurate, and then suddenly becomes the opposite: mean and manipulative. Sometimes there is a change of personalities: the nice entity leaves and is replaced by a negative entity that is able to move right in and have a hold on a person. The victim undergoes a deterioration of health, mental oppression, nightmarish sleep, inability to concentrate, and so on. The atmosphere of the home changes as well, to gloomy, heavy, and depressing. The victim may feel watched by unseen, hostile eyes.

Zozo has a similar pattern. Many people report that Zozo is nice at first, even helpful, describing itself as an angel of light or a guardian angel—only later revealing its true intentions. Sometimes Zozo is preceded by an introductory act of friendly-sounding spirits that will communicate for a while, and then warn of Zozo's arrival. When Zozo surfaces, there is a definite change in the planchette behavior on a spirit board. The movements become much quicker and faster. In many instances, Zozo will immediately show its trademark "rainbow effect" of scooting back and forth between the Z and O. Users also report that the whole atmosphere changes dramatically in the room, and a negative presence can be felt. Some users black out, fall into a deep trance, or undergo behavioral changes.

### The Infernal Dictionary

If Zozo is a demon, then where are its historical tracks? Critics point to the lack of Zozo's name in important lists of demons and magical handbooks, or grimoires, such as *The Lemegeton*.

Zozo is mentioned in the *Dictionnaire Infernal*, a classic reference work on demons written by Jacques Albin Simon Collin de Plancy (1793-1887), a printer and publisher in Plancy l'Abbaye and Paris. Between 1830 and 1837, Collin de Plancy lived in Brussels, and then returned to France after it returned to the Catholic religion, and lived there for the rest of his life.

Interested in the occult and superstitions, Collin de Plancy wrote dozens of books under pseudonyms on divination, magic, alchemy, sorcery, and witchcraft. About eighty volumes alone were devoted to superstitions. Prolific, he earned a comfortable living.

His most famous, significant, and enduring work is the *Dictionnaire Infernal (Infernal Dictionary or Dictionary of Demonology)*, published under his real name in two volumes in 1818. The dictionary profiles demons and gives short summaries of notable cases and trials of witchcraft and sorcery, as well as summaries of ghosts and odd paranormal events. The dictionary went through several editions. In 1863, the artist Louis Breton created a set of sixty-nine drawings, all but five of them of demons, which were engraved by a man named M. Jarrault. Collin de Plancy added them to his book.

While scouring the *Dictionnaire Infernal*, Darren found a mention of Zozo as a demon (in some translations, "imp") that had played a role in a French possession case involving a young girl in 1816. According to Collin de Plancy, the case involved three demons, Mimi, Crapoulet, and Zozo. The following translation was made for us by Marion Nobu:

> In 1816, the Picardie region has been an area of a scandalous case of demonic possession. In the village of Teilly, near the city of Amiens, a girl got pregnant, and to hide this accident, she managed to publish that she was possessed by three devilkins: Mimi, Zozo, and Crapoulet. Crapoulet could be involved in the affair because it is a good "philanderer."
>
> Anyway, the girl Beth... went on the streets on all fours, sometimes forward, sometimes backward, and sometimes she walked on her hands, feet in the air, at the risk of revealing her pregnancy to the citizens. Mimi pushed her forward, Zozo pulled her backward, and the malignant Crapoulet held her legs in the air. An old son of Loyola [a Jesuit], in the runway of good adventures, and who recognized the devils to good intuition, seized the girl and performed an exorcism.
>
> Mimi went out without noise, Zozo was more persistent, and broke a stained glass window of the

church by escaping on the rooftops, and Crapoulet, it was in vain that we pursued it, by taking a stand in the girl's genitalia. The girl left the neighborhood of this place with discretion, and under the protection of the Jesuit.

This reference to Zozo as a demon is disturbing to some, because Collin de Plancy's book was written about eighty years before the invention of the Ouija board, thus contradicting the argument that Zozo is strictly a modern, board-created phenomenon.

As noted earlier, Zozo's behavior often focuses on sexual perversion and attraction to females, especially teenage girls, during spirit board sessions. Sexual attack from demonic entities is not a subject openly discussed, yet historical and even modern records document incubus and succubus attacks on women and men. The attacks often occur in a dream or lucid state, but some individuals experience them while fully conscious. Victims describe being sexually aroused before drifting off to sleep, but soon things turn quickly into a nightmare of molestation. Victims may feel a heavy weight on their bodies and feel depressions by invisible presences on their beds. Physical symptoms include scratches, bruises, and cuts. Some victims admit to enjoying the experience, but most are left with emotions of guilt and shame.

In Darren's research, he found that sexual experiences sometimes became more frequent after the victim had repeated communication with Zozo or any of the Z-entities. This repeated sexual communication between Zozo and young females continues to be just one of the disturbing aspects of this phenomenon. Dozens of teenagers and pre-teens have contacted Darren, terrified as a result of conversations with Zozo in which the entity threatened to rape them, along with other vile exchanges.

Robert Murch has received Zozo stories from board players, and shared two sexual ones with us. Murch, as you recall, was featured on the *Ghost Adventures* board episode. He brought along two boards from his collection, one of which was used in the filming.

That board came from a man who was seventeen at the time of his extreme experiences. He played with the board for the first time on a Halloween night and took the board home. That night, he felt his pants being pulled down and then an invisible something performed oral sex on him. It happened again the next night. Every night he had vivid dreams. He got scared and gave the board to a girl he knew, and the next day she returned it to him because she had felt herself being touched in the night. He shipped the board to Murch, and there were no more visits. Murch, by the way, has more than six hundred Ouija boards in his collection, and has never been bothered or haunted.

The second board, which was not used on the show, was a 1990s Ouija owned by a young woman. In May 2007, when she was a teenager, she attended a friend's birthday party and joined in board playing. It was all in fun, with the girls asking such questions as who was going to get married. The next day, she visited her grandmother. She explored the attic she found the Ouija board, and took it home. She was secretive about using it, waiting until her parents went out for the night. The first time she asked the board if anyone was present, she received the answer, YES. Asking for a name, the planchette spelled ZOZO.

At first, the communications with Zozo were lighthearted. She played with the board daily whenever she had free time. That summer, she got a job at a store in a shopping mall and met a boy who worked as a stock clerk, and started dating him. Zozo got jealous and started pranking on him. The young man experienced weird accidents, for example, boxes that were secured on upper shelves in the stockroom would tumble down.

Zozo became ugly. It told the girl that it was going to get her pregnant and she would have a deformed baby. A few weeks later, she took a pregnancy test and the results were positive. Then Zozo told her it was going to possess the baby. She and her boyfriend finally had enough. They took the board outside her house, intending to burn it, but then changed their minds, afraid that the action would make Zozo angrier. The girl suffered a miscarriage.

We can speculate that the pregnancy may have been a natural one, not supernatural, but nonetheless, Zozo knew about it and proclaimed it before the girl knew it. Was Zozo acting like a demon with foreknowledge—or was the board communication mirroring the girl's projected subconscious concern that she might be pregnant? Either way, she was terrified, and got rid of the board.

## A saint's sermon

A remarkable demonic reference to Zozo is found in a sermon by the Franciscan saint, Bernadino of Siena, who lived from 1380-1444. St. Bernadino was known as the "apostle of Italy" for his travels about the land delivering stern sermons. He once told a crowd that he would show them devils, and then shocked everyone by telling them to look at each other, for they were doing the work of Satan.

In one of St. Bernadino's Lent sermons, he lashed out against gaming, considered a vice by the Church. Bernadino was renowned for entertaining his audiences during his sermons, and he delivered his message by hypothesizing what would happen if the Devil himself set up his own church of gaming and measured itself, feature by feature, against the church of Christ. The story of this sermon is recounted in *The Month and Catholic Review*, a Catholic publication dated 1876.

According to Bernadino's scenario, the Devil would become the Supreme Pontiff of his gaming church, with all his devils in attendance, and wicked, corrupt, and greedy human authorities would serve as religious figures such as cardinals and bishops. The missal—traditionally a book containing the texts of masses—would instead be a dice box. According to *The Month*:

> When he comes to the services and vestments of the new Church, St. Bernadine travels somewhat beyond our intelligence in his details, but they must have been very intelligible, and must have sounded very racy to an audience in an Italian town... As the Christian saints have masses of their own, so certain particularly eminent devils are to have their own masses in this new order of things. These devils are named apparently after the various throws of the dice, which had names of their own— Testa, Sbatalio, Sbaralio, Minoreta, Sequentia, Spagnolo riverso, Badolos, and Rapello. The "mass of Zozo" is to be the "commune omnium daemonum" ["common to all the demons"]. The "mass of Zarro" is to be like the Sunday mass of the Christians, and reserved for the impious Majesty himself.

St. Bernadino did not elaborate on the details of "the mass of Zozo," and a search of his sermons did not yield any other references to either Zozo or Zarro. What is significant, however, is that this is a religious reference to Zozo with a demonic connection—made about five hundred years before the arrival of the spirit board.

It is important to find the historical references to Zozo as a demon, but even without them, the testimonies of experiencers stand on their own. Demons are shapeshifters, so it is cannot be ruled out that they use multiple names over the course of time.

## Djinn

Zozo also exhibits the characteristics of some powerful beings in the supernatural realm, the Djinn. Their name in Arabic means "Hidden Ones," and the Djinn like to hide behind many names, faces, and shapes when they interact with human beings. They are masterful shapeshifters. Most of the lore about Djinn originates in the Middle East, but like all supernatural beings, the Djinn are everywhere on Earth and are not limited by human religions or cultures.

According to their creation stories, the Djinn once had dominion over the Earth, but lost it to humans. They retreated to another world. In ancient times it was believed to be underground, and in modern terms could be explained as a parallel or alternate dimension. They are still present on the planet, but invisible to people most of the time. They are well-known in many parts of the world, but less so in the West, where they are primarily known by a corrupted translation of their name, genie. Our lack of knowledge about them does not mean we have no encounters with them—we do.

The Djinn, like humans, have a range of dispositions, but it seems the ones who seek out the most interaction with people do not like human beings, even hate them. They are capable of everything ascribed to demons: hauntings, poltergeist disturbances, attachments, nightmares, sexual attacks, and varying stages of oppression and possession. They are renowned for their deceitfulness and their lust for vengeance and blood. Some of them attach to people and follow them for years, even lifetimes, remaining hidden for long periods, and then manifesting in an instant when it suits them. They can be quite possessive of humans, and disrupt their victims' relationships with friends, spouses, and lovers—just as Zozo disrupted the relationship described previously.

The Djinn are said to be ruled by kings—and Zozo frequently proclaims itself to be the "king of kings." The arrogance displayed by Zozo is often displayed in Djinn encounters: they consider themselves to be far superior to humans. Zozo often enjoys toying with people, another characteristic of many Djinn encounters.

The following account actually mentions a term for a type of low-level Djinn called *hinn*. The term is spelled HIN on the board—it is common for shorthand spellings and even misspellings to occur in board communications. We cannot say for certain that "Hin" is a reference to Djinn, but it fits the profile:

> My name is Cherie and I am nineteen. My friend Jake and I have been having some very strange occurrences happening in our apartment. Jake had his head bashed into a mirror, had his foot grabbed to the point of it almost yanking him out of the bed, my bed has been lifted on the corner, I see dark figures walking through the hallways. It just kept escalating. Finally, I turned to using a Ouija board for help. I just wanted to know who or what else was living in our home.
>
> I had used a board before, so it was no problem for me. I am well aware that some of the spirits that like to manipulate the board are just trying to have some fun with us or manipulate us in some way. Once the name Zozo came up it was downhill from there. This spirit told us that he wanted to kill Jake, harm me, but would leave our other roommate and her son alone. He also told us that he resides in our apartment and that there are two others there as well, something/someone called Hin and Diablo himself. Zozo claims that Diablo is living inside of Jake and that he is just waiting until the day he can take over Earth itself. That Josh is supposed to reproduce to fill the earth with "satanic spawn."
>
> Things got pretty intense to the point that the planchette would point to Jake and attempt to fly off of the board towards him. It also stated that I am supposed to kill my friend Jen. After that we decided to put the board

away. We told the spirits goodbye and put the board back in the box, put it in the top of my closet, and put a suitcase in front of it.

This afternoon, after I left for work, Jake woke up and the board was sitting next to him. There was also loud banging coming from our other roommate's room, and Jake was seeing figures throughout the apartment. After that he left and went to a friend's house. Jake states that the figures followed him there as well. He can see and hear them walking around. Josh and I are so scared that we have both been sleeping in the living room so we won't have to be alone.

What are we supposed to do to get rid of whatever is in our home?? And can this Zozo entity really hurt us? And should we believe that the Devil or Diablo is really in our home? Please help.

The *hinn* are low on the Djinn totem pole, a type that especially likes to appear in the form of dogs. It is also significant that Zozo says he is waiting until the day he can take over the Earth—a very Djinn agenda.

In this case, the Arabic *hinn* is paired with the Spanish term for devil, *diablo*. This mixing fits the behavior of Zozo: predictable in its unpredictability.

Djinn make themselves known by poltergeist phenomena such as thumps and bangs on ceilings and walls; clumping, heavy footsteps; cold breezes and winds; and disappearing and reappearing objects. They often like to leave old, scarred coins in odd places, usually pennies, nickels, and dimes. Many of our Zozo cases describe these phenomena.

The masquerading done by Zozo is another Djinn trait. Zozo has disguised itself as children, dead loved ones, angels, higher intelligence beings, monstrous animal forms as noted above, demons, and even the Devil. They are especially fond of manifesting in dark shadow forms such as silhouettes of men, blobs, pillars of black, and spider-like masses that crawl along. They also appear as snakes, and as black-eyed children and adults, appearing either in solid or ghostly form. The skinned man who hunched like a dog/monkey, described in the previous chapter, is a good example of a Djinn form.

When Djinn attack sleeping people at night, they apply crushing pressure to the chest—a phenomenon in earlier times ascribed to witches and demons, and called the Old Hag. Scratches and bruises may appear on the bodies of victims.

The disguises do not last long—Zozo seems to enjoy revealing its real self.

In the following account, a Scottish woman describes encountering a crawling black "person/thing" while astral travelling—and then has the name "Zozo" embedded in her mind:

Hello my name is Heather. I'm from Edinburgh in Scotland. I've been sensitive since a near-death experience at thirteen. Now I have had a strange experience last night. I haven't played with a Ouija board since I was a kid and never contacted anything like this. The only connection I've really had with demonic or even satanic stuff was as a child (it's difficult to talk about but if you think it's relevant I'll try to).

I astral travel a bit, not much but a little. I did this last night. I saw something very big, dark and almost crawling sometimes. It followed me and I tried to see its face and asked what it wanted, to which this person/thing just laughed and said it had been with me for a while. The only other thing I got from it was the word "mine" as I felt almost a crushing sensation in my chest. I got this horrible feeling that my physical body was being disturbed (don't know what you know or believe when it comes to travelling but I'm very in tune with my physical body and will rush back if I feel this).

Anyway, I woke up and I could not get this word/name "Zozo" out of my head, I was covered in sweat, was lying on my front (this is extremely weird for me as I have had a lot of surgery on my tummy, so I can't sleep on my front, it's way too painful if I'm like that for longer than ten minutes). The other weird thing was, I felt like I'd worked out, and (this is a bit embarrassing) my underwear were down to my knees, also have scratches on my back which I'm going to get a decent picture taken when someone else gets home (sorry, this literally just happened).

Since I woke up, I've been violently sick and I'm actually having to go and see my specialist because it looks like my Crohn's Disease has flared up out of nowhere. It might be nothing, it might be something else. Can this entity come to people or even follow them for many years, then appear like this? I said at the start that I was non-consensually involved in pretty grim stuff, which I've dealt with memory-wise as best I can. Could that be responsible?

I've also been unwell for many years since the satanic stuff and just very unsure. It's probably nothing, but as I couldn't get that name out my head I Googled it and found your [Darren's] site.

Heather's description is characteristic of a Djinn encounter. They can navigate the astral plane, and do not need a spirit board to approach people. The board may have opened the door, and the astral traveling completed the vulnerability.

Djinn also are drawn to dark occult work such as demon summoning, which carries a risk of attachment. As mentioned, they may lie dormant for long periods of time before striking.

The boundaries between Djinn and demons blur considerably, so it is often difficult to determine one from the other. Is Zozo a demon or a Djinn? Perhaps it is a bit of both.

## A collective

Are the Z-entities and alternate names all tied to a single Zozo—or is Zozo actually part of a collective or a group of entities that share the same pool? Earlier, we recounted experiencer stories in which Zozo or a Z-entity refers to one of the other alter egos.

Many spirits and demons, as well as the Djinn, have the ability to manifest in multiple forms. Rosemary has observed this is some of the Djinn and demon cases she has investigated, in which they appear alternately as mysterious creatures, moving lights, shadow figures, apparitions, and monstrous forms.

Zozo may have the ability to similarly project multiple identities that can even carry on conversations among themselves.

We cannot rule out a collective entity, either. For example, in the channeling literature, "Ra," channeled by Carla Rueckert, describes itself as a collective. In instrumental transcommunication (ITC) research, which seeks technology bridges to the afterlife and spirit world, researchers have been contacted by collective entities. However, in both of these situations, the collective speaks with a single voice and identity and refers to itself in first person plural, "we." In general, the collective makes contact for the purpose of teaching and enlightenment, not harassment, though the ITC literature documents problems suffered by researchers following contact with certain collectives as well as individual communicators. In her book *Talking to the Dead* (2011), co-authored with George Noory, Rosemary documents some of those cases, which involved disturbing poltergeist phenomena, demonic voices, threatening messages, and deteriorations of mental and physical health.

A prototypical example of a demonic collective is found in the Bible. The Gospels of Mark, Luke, and Matthew tell how Jesus exorcized a possessed man, a Gerasene, soon after delivering his Sermon on the Mount:

> For He [Jesus] had been saying to him [the spirit], "Come out of the man, you unclean spirit!" And He was asking him, "What is your name?" And he said to Him, "My name is Legion; for we are many." (Mark 5:8-10)

Legion then begged Jesus not to send them out of the country. Instead, Jesus drove the devils into about two thousand swine, who became possessed and rushed down a cliff into the sea and drowned.

Is Zozo like Legion—one of many entities in a collective, all of whom band together to behave and attack in certain ways? If they are part of a group, do they compete with each other—or are those just shows for people? We mentioned earlier that the Z-entities and Mama make a display of arguing and fighting for control of the board. Here is another example, from a woman who said she is a medium, empath, and shaman. She had never before heard of Zozo or Mama until they showed up on the talking board, and then she became convinced they were demons:

I have encountered Zozo and Mama in the same session…. The last day of this past full moon period, January 10, 2012, my brother and I used my Ouija board that I have had since I was in high school, though it is was tucked in my parent's closet since high school. I haven't touched it until last week—I am now thirty-eight years old.

What spurred my interest in touching this thing again was a recent visit of two demons to me after putting a request—a summons, if you will—to confirm my intuition on which demon terrorized me for years when I was thirteen to nineteen years old. I sealed my house and they went away—this was during the first night of three of the past full moon period. I needed to know who they were and…. do research. Because I have had so much activity at a young age, and have developed residual skills, I have recently chosen to write an autobiographical trilogy about my first experiences with the paranormal, hence the delay in asking (see below on my hesitance).

I have had numerous, and I mean numerous, experiences on this board and other Ouija boards, never once did I meet Zozo or Mama, nor have I heard of these demons, despite my intensive research. Back in the '80s we didn't have the luxury of the internet and there was very little accessible research, so I learned through experience, and well…. let's just say I got into a lot of trouble. My mother's grandmother was shaman (Native American), my mom is shaman, and I am shaman, which is how when I was nineteen years old my mom helped me, through ritual, strip my powers and completely block my intuition. It was getting so intense and I couldn't keep up with the development of my abilities to know how to control them, I just got too scared. Now…… I became a Reiki Master in 1999 and since then my intuition and powers are returning, though not at the level they once were. They are, however, getting close and now I have additional, different abilities. They are growing every day, but I am blessed with the ability to guard myself and somewhat control them.

With that albeit brief introduction to me and the context of the incident that occurred on January 10, 2012, here is what happened:

I dusted off the thick layer of dust on the Ouija board and placed it between me and my brother, who, incidentally, is also intuitive. I did not light candles nor play death metal, as in the video [a video found on the internet]. My intentions were not to provoke anything. We sat on the floor and placed the board on a small ottoman between us. I sealed the room, but left a small portal open, knowing that to get answers I needed, I probably would need to talk to a negative entity. I grounded and shielded both me and my brother and then placed our fingertips on the board.

It started up immediately. I wasn't surprised. That happened every time I touched even a homemade board. It made oval circles (I was looking for figure eights, four corners, etc., indicators of an evil presence). I asked for Danny, a ghost that followed and protected me when I was being terrorized younger. Then it moved back and forth from Z to O. I knew it wasn't Danny, and I was not angry.

I asked, "Who is this?" It went back and forth between Z and O faster. I asked, "What are you?" It darted between Z and O. I asked, "Zo? What is Zo?" It wouldn't answer, just kept going back and forth. I said, "That is OK, thank you for visiting us." I asked if it would answer some questions. It said YES.

I asked if Asmodeus was at least partially responsible for the hauntings and experiences I had [before]. It said YES. I said, "Thank you."

Then I asked again, "Who are you?" It slowed a second, then went back and forth to M and A. I said, "Mama?" It went to YES. I asked, "What are you?" It slowed then went to NO, then back to Z and O.

At that point I knew that two entities were fighting for the board and that Zo (at that time I didn't know it was "Zozo") didn't want Mama to answer certain questions. Which is understandable. They like to keep secrets, or rather, especially demons like to keep secrets.

I asked, "Are you a demon?" It slowed, but wouldn't answer. Then Mama showed up and it dashed to YES. I asked if she was a demon. It slowed and Zozo showed up and was *pissed.* I said, "It is okay, I already knew. Shhhhh... It is okay. Thank you for visiting me. I will be closing the portal but appreciate your visit." It went to GOODBYE, and my brother and I just looked at each other for a bit...

Now, I will do the same thing I said to my brother when I talked to him about this, I swear on my parents' graves (both are alive and I am very close to them), I have never heard of Zozo or Mama.

As mentioned earlier, most people who are familiar with Zozo consider it to be a demon. The entity certainly knows that by giving that identity, the average board user will become frightened, and if there is an appearance of multiple entities, fear is likely to escalate.

Deception is one the hallmarks of Zozo, so how can we believe it, no matter who or what it claims to be?

## The demons within

In his novel *The Brothers Karamazov* (1880), Fyodor Dostoyevsky observes, "In every man, of course, a demon lies hidden—the demon of rage, the demon of lustful heat at the screams of the tortured victim, the demon of lawlessness let off the chain." Is Zozo a projection of the darkness that lies within the human soul?

All human beings are capable of committing horrific acts, including murder, but only a very small percentage of people ever act out in such ways. Are there malicious demons inside all people that push for expression in some way? Do humans have a dark side that has the capability of taking on its own external personality ? The occultist and ceremonial magician Aleister Crowley believed that the Goetic spirits—the seventy-two demons (Djinn) under the command of the legendary King Solomon—reside within the human brain.

Psychologist Carl G. Jung said, "If, for a moment we look at mankind as one individual, we see that it is like a man carried away by unconscious powers." The psychic conditions that breed demons are as actively at work as ever in history. The demons have never disappeared, but have merely taken on another form. They have become unconscious psychic forces.

Are we all capable of being taken over by our personal demons? Does the spirit board help facilitate the manifestation of dangerous psychic forces? Perhaps we all bound by a common dark thread that originates squarely with us.

## Archetypes and the shadow side

Earlier in this chapter we touched on the concept of archetypes. Jung developed this concept, which originated in ancient Greek philosophy. Jung described archetypes as the contents of the collective unconsciousness, a reservoir of memories and mental patterns shared by humans throughout history. The archetypes are primordial images passed down from humanity primordial past, and also its prehumen and animal ancestors. All of us contribute to the collective unconscious every day with our thoughts, actions, beliefs, and emotions.

Jung said that archetypes are not conscious thoughts, but are predispositions toward certain behaviors, such as fear of the dark. The trickster is an example of an archetype. Jung said that archetypes are potentially unlimited in number, and they are powerful psychic forces that demand attention and need to be taken seriously.

Furthermore, Jung identified four major archetypes that play significant roles in human behavior. The persona is our public mask, the face we present to others. The anima/animus are the female and male sides of every psyche, regardless of gender. The self is the organizing principle of the personality that unites the conscious and unconscious. And finally, of significance to our discussion here, is the shadow, the inferior "other" side of a person.

The shadow exists in the personal unconscious. It is uncivilized and desires that which is not allowed by the persona, or by society. It is that which is despised and rejected. The shadow remains primitive and repressed throughout life, but pops up in dreams in the form of crude, unlikeable, and even violent dream figures. The shadow also appears in fantasies and delusions.

If Zozo is at least in part a thoughtform created by collective human energy, perhaps it also is a projection of the human shadow—the part of us that fears the dark, fears evil, and secretly wishes to act out in unacceptable ways, such as through deceit and sexual aggression.

Serial killers and other violent criminals have sometimes described the voices in their heads that prompted them to commit heinous crimes. These voices seemed to be independent, such as might come from a possessing entity—but how many of them might be projections of the demons within? There is no definitive line to be drawn. It may not be a case of one or the other, but both.

## Synchronicity

Jung also developed—but did not originate—the concept of synchronicity, or "meaningful coincidences." Synchronicity occurs when seemingly unrelated events are linked in a meaningful way. It can be highly subjective, that is, of personal significance to an individual.

Jung said synchronicity can occur with the alignment of "universal forces" with the life experiences of an individual. He believed that many experiences such as coincidences were not merely due to chance, but instead reflected the creation of an event or circumstance by the "coinciding" or alignment of such forces.

Could the Zozo Phenomenon also involve synchronicity on a mass scale—an organization of forces involving human thought, thoughtforms, shadow archetype projections, fear, desire, board activity, and so on, all rolled into one? Could this account for the many independent experiences of Zozo, shared by people who never heard the name before it was spelled out on their board?

Perhaps events in the outer world—even encounters with entities such as Zozo—are at least in part symbolic reflections of what resides within us. Perhaps our consciousness is the real spirit board.

## The mystery of Zozo

It may not be possible to precisely identify or define Zozo beyond its trademarks behavior patterns. Thoughtform, demon, Djinn, shadow, inner demon—it could be a mixture of all of those. It also may be yet something else we have not discovered—an unknown interdimensional being.

Whatever Zozo is, it is real, and it is capable of manifesting all over the world. The fact that Zozo can manifest simultaneously in many places does not necessarily mean that it is really multiple entities. Spirits of all kinds, including angels and demons, exhibit the ability to be anywhere at any time, even multiple locations.

Thanks to the internet and social media, we can continue to collect data on Zozo. Its characteristics and mannerisms show its negative agenda regardless of race, color, gender, nationality, or geographical location of its victims. If Zozo is an entity, does it have a master plan in the works beyond mere pestering?

The various threads connecting so many aspects of Zozo still do not yield a complete picture, and to the mystery continues.

# 12

## Strange Encounters

People do not have to be spirit board users to be adversely affected by Zozo. Some victims are spectators during sessions. Some are not using boards, but other devices to contact the spirit realm. Zozo finds many other ways to link to people, as the stories in this chapter illustrate—some of them with serious consequences.

### Blood red

This account comes from a concerned mother:

> This happened to my daughter, starting when she was twelve. Her friends had watched some Zozo videos on YouTube while on an educational trip to Washington, D.C. The girls were all staying in one hotel room, and the adult chaperones (as her mom, I was also a chaperone) were in a different room.

One of the girls got the idea that they should try to communicate with Zozo. Although they did not have a Ouija board, the girls all sat in a circle in a dark room, and one of them said, "If Zozo is here, show us a sign of something red." At that moment, my daughter got a terrible nosebleed which took several minutes to stop. All the girls were shaken up, but they tried to get some sleep since we had a busy day the next day.

My daughter was lying in the bed with her friend, and her friend started shaking in her sleep very violently—almost like a seizure. The girls woke up her friend and ran to get a chaperone who is also a nurse. She managed to calm this girl down, but her eyes were very glassy, and she didn't seem like herself.

The girls tried to sleep again, but all claim to have seen upside down crosses on the wall and an apparition of a girl with braided hair who was wearing a dirty white dress.

Honestly, I blew them off, but I told them to stop "playing" with spirits as no good could come from it.

After we returned home, my daughter started complaining of dark shadows flitting around in the ceiling corners of her bedroom, and she claimed to hear a voice call her name. I gave her a font of holy water for her bedroom and told her to pray if it happened. At this point, I didn't really believe anything real was happening, but I thought the holy water and prayers might help with what I thought was an overactive imagination.

A few months later, my daughter had to have extensive surgery to repair her ACL and meniscus in her right knee. Before the surgery, she complained of the shadow activity intensifying. Again, I blew it off.

Well, what should have been a routine surgery became a nightmare. Although her doctor was top notch, she developed an extremely rare klebsiella pneumoniae infection (1 in 1000 odds) at the surgical site. Despite her constant fever and numerous trips to the ER, it wasn't detected until three weeks later. The ER docs misread her lab report. It took her pediatrician noticing the abnormally high CRP levels to know that she had a serious problem. All the while, she was still seeing these shadows.

She ended up being admitted for emergency surgery to "wash out" her knee. The doctor had to flush her knee with nine liters of antibiotic fluid. We had to consult with an infectious disease specialist, and she had to have a PICC line placed in her arm so she could receive an eight-week course of daily intravenous antibiotic infusions.

At this point, we'd put her name on our parish's prayer list and had many people (including everyone at the Catholic school she attends) praying for her. She had an extremely rare fever reaction to the first intravenous antibiotic the doctor tried. We were very fortunate that her infection responded to the second antibiotic treatment.

At the end of her ordeal, she was left with a much smaller, much weaker right leg. She missed over a month of school. Her skin was unbelievably pale, and blue veining was evident. She had bags under her eyes, and she had allergic reactions to the tape used on her skin. It took months of physical therapy to get her close to her pre-surgery state. Today, she is much better!

Since then, she says she still sees the shadows occasionally, but it has subsided. I have a blessed crucifix hanging outside her bedroom door, and she has the St. Michael the Archangel prayer posted on her bulletin board. She prays that prayer whenever she sees the shadows.

I have ordered a St. Michael medal for her to wear, and I plan to have a priest bless our house in the near future. (Honestly, I am worried at what our parish priest might say if I tell him this story. It sounds quite far-fetched. That's why I haven't sought his help yet.)

Anyway, this is my daughter's story. Although there was no Ouija board involved, I have no doubt that she and her friends opened the door to demonic spirits when they asked Zozo to show its presence. I also believe she was (and still is, to a lesser degree) being harassed by them. Praying to St. Michael has helped.

## Dream invasion

One of the most insidious forms of negative entity attack comes via dreams. The victim suffers from repeated, violent dreams often involving bloodshed and being pursued by monsters. These dreams are distinctly different from ordinary dreams that are nightmarish and related to personal matters.

> I am sending this email to relate my experiences to you. My experiences are not Ouija related but dream related. My first experience was in during the late summer of 1988. With the end of summer approaching and the beginning of school on the horizon the usual depression started to set in. Constantly bullied and picked on at school led to me literally being filled with dread.
>
> A few days before the first day of the school year (my fifth grade year) I sat in my room literally terrified of the thoughts of being bullied and picked on. At bed time I said out loud that I wish someone could help me. That night I had a dream where a shadow figure who introduced himself as Zozo told me that he could help me, but I in turn would have to help him. I agreed and asked how he could help me and stop the other kids from bullying me and he simply said do as I ask and it will be done. My part of the deal was to take a book from one of my teachers and destroy it (granted we did not receive our class schedule until the next morning).
>
> Lo and behold the next morning I received my schedule and the teacher that Zozo spoke about was on my schedule and I had her class after lunch. Now this teacher (a very young and extremely religious woman) had just graduated college and accepted the position and moved to our small town two months earlier. I had never met her or heard of her until that day. That day I arrived in her class twenty minutes early (I would skip recess to hide from being picked on). I was the only one in the class and on her book shelf was the book Zozo mentioned in my dream. EXACTLY as he described it... a large brown old book with a chain clasp.

I took the book, placed it in my backpack and placed it in my locker. I went and hid in the bathroom waiting for the bell to ring to announce recess was over. Luckily she didn't notice the book was missing and I went home with it.

Zozo was adamant about burning the book. We had burn barrels we used to burn trash, so I placed it in the barrel and covered it with a few bags of trash. My father on schedule burned the trash that evening.

That night Zozo once again visited me in my dreams and praised me for holding up my end of the deal. He then promised that the main kid who bullied me would never bother me again. Zozo then told me that he would return in one year and visit me again.

The next morning, we were gathered and taken into the auditorium. There we were told that one of our classmates [the bully] was hit by a car while riding his bike to school. He was in the hospital for four months and was wheelchair bound after the accident. The book I took and burned (I found out later) was an antique Catholic prayer book.

Zozo did return a year later.

It feels so good to get this off of my chest. Hopefully you can perhaps shed some light on what I experienced.

Interestingly, Zozo's dream invasion, deal-making, and severe consequences are major hallmarks of Djinn behavior.

## A telepathic connection

This strange case involves a telepathic connection between two people using a talking board and another person at a distant location, who communicated on the board that he was asleep. The entire event may have been to amuse Zozo:

Way back in 1978 (junior year in college, Western MA) I had a genuine telepathy experience involving a Ouija board and a good friend from high school who was at school about 500 miles away. Was fooling around with the board one afternoon, and the friend identified himself, said that he was asleep, and added a couple of statements that didn't make sense until later. The last one was "make Zozo laugh," which we never figured out.

Right after that I ran for the phone and after a couple calls, found out he'd been very ill, recovering, and his brother and sister-in-law had just gotten home from the airport, after putting him on a plane to his parents in Florida.

I wrote the whole thing down in my diary at the time and we confirmed later that my friend been asleep on the plane while my roommate and I were using the board.

That was the last time I used a Ouija board... This entity may have been around for quite a long time.

Telepathic communication among the living in distant locations is not unheard of in board use, and often is benign in nature. In this case, however, Zozo seems to have inserted itself in the situation for its own amusement.

## Automatic writing

In the next account, Zozo manifested in automatic writing, a technique in which a person asks questions and allows spirits to write answers through their hands. The experiencer, a woman, is another victim who referred to Zozo as a "she."

Hello. My name is Hillary. I had just found your website about Zozo and I decided to tell you about my experiences. I had met her [Zozo] through an Auto Writing Session with my brother while we tried to contact our grandmother. Instantly stuff had been happening. Objects were being moved and thrown around the room. The candle was rapidly flickering. And I had been scratched on the chest. She had kept trying to get either my brother or my girlfriend at the time to commit suicide because she wanted them. Neither of them did so this made her mad. She manifested into a black shadow and all of a sudden all of the doors in the room swung open and then slammed shut. It was the scariest experience of my life. Since then we burned the notebook and haven't done anything like that. But we didn't say goodbye. We looked it up and realized we were supposed to say goodbye and have her say it back. So I guess it kinda explains the doors slamming and everything since that night.

## Ghost boxes

Rosemary has encountered Zozo while using ghost boxes, which are radio sweep devices popular in paranormal investigation that are intended to facilitate real-time, two-way communication across the veil. In those cases of hers, Zozo usually surfaces during investigations of intensely haunted places, especially those that have had a negative, violent, or troubled history.

Ghost boxes scan the radio band in a rapid way to generate a noise jumble, sounds picked up by a second or so of radio broadcast as the sweep passes through the band. The jumbled noise facilitates Electronic Voice Phenomena (EVP)—rather like providing a sound background for spirit voices to manifest and shape words. EVP research has been going on since the nineteenth century, when researchers accidentally discovered "mystery voices" in the background of telegraphy and radio transmissions, and, later, in magnetic tape recordings. In traditional EVP research, a recording device is turned on, questions are asked, and then the recording is played back to see if unheard answers were captured.

Ghost boxes facilitate real-time communication—answers can be heard on the box. Ghosts boxes have been in use in various forms for more than fifty years, but became especially popular within the past decade. Most ghost boxes scan the AM band, because AM stations have more talk than FM stations. The ability of the boxes to perform well depends heavily upon the number of stations the box can pick up in any given location. The more stations, the better the scan.

Most communications that come over the box are short—a word or two, perhaps several at the most. This may be due to the limitations of the scan itself. The links also tend to be short: after a few exchanges, the connection drops. There are some cases where the exchange is lengthy, but the majority are limited. The voices speak in an unusual cadence, usually clipped, which may also be a by-product of the scan.

Ghost boxes have sometimes been called "electronic Ouija boards." Their results are often controversial, due to the indistinct nature of many of the communications, and to the hazard of misinterpreting random broadcast words as EVP.

Communicators identifying themselves as Djinn have shown up in many of Rosemary's ghost box sessions, perhaps because she has devoted a great deal of time for years to researching them. When they do appear, they are, like Zozo, derisive and crude. Sometimes a Djinn communicator will give its name as Zozo or Zaza. These exchanges never produce anything of value in terms of information. Once the nameless Djinn or Zozo appears, the session takes a turn and Rosemary asks them to depart. If they do not, she ends the session and shuts off the device.

Here is an example of a short ghost box exchange, recorded at an investigation on a private property. It often takes a few minutes for communication to be established. In this case, a male-sounding voice finally appeared. The transcript is the only survivor of this exchange. The audio file became corrupted.

> REG: Who is communicating, please?
> (A sound like unh!)
> REG: Who is communicating, please?
> Voice: Djinn.
> REG: Djinn? Did you say Djinn?
> Voice: Djinn.
> REG: Do you have a name? What is your name?
> (No response.)
> REG: Name, please. What is your name?
> Voice: Zozo! (Said very rapidly and as an exclamation.)
> REG: You are Zozo? Confirm, please.
> Voice: Yes.
> REG: Zozo, what are you doing here?
> Voice: Hate.
> REG: Hate? Who or what do you hate?
> (Indistinguishable)

REG: Do you hate someone in this house?
Voice: [Expletive.]
REG: You can answer questions or go.
Voice: [Expletive.]
REG: Leave immediately.
Voice: No.
REG: Leave immediately.
(No response.)
REG: You are not welcome here. Leave now.
(No response.)
REG: This session is ended.
(Device shut off.)

Abusive exchanges should always be terminated, regardless of the device being used. Many board users get hooked on the drama and thrill and allow negative entities like Zozo too much freedom.

# 13

# The Disturbing Letter Z

The letter Z affects people in odd ways. Names that start with Z are rare and exotic, and immediately evoke both curiosity and dread. Perhaps that is why one of the most feared entities of the talking board revels in Z names—because they are instant attention-grabbers.

The strange and troubled history of the letter Z may shed light on the personality and behavior of Zozo and its Z-entities alter egos.

## The whoreson zed

Z, or Zed as it is known in British English, has always had a problematic, even shady, reputation. It has been the least used and lowest regarded of all the letters of the Latin alphabet. Perhaps the greatest insult to Z came from William Shakespeare. In his play *King Lear*, Act Two Scene Three, the character Kent insults a man by comparing him to the letter Z: "Thou whoreson zed, thou unnecessary letter!"

"Whoreson" means "an unpleasant or greatly disliked person," or, in blunter terms, a "useless bastard."

Throughout history, it seems we have not known what to do with Z. The letter is derived from the Greek term *zeta*, only one of two letters in the Latin alphabet that came from Greek instead of Etruscan. *Zeta* derived from Semitic languages, chiefly the Phoenician *zayin*, which means "weapon." The glyph had a long vertical line capped at both ends with shorter stubbier horizontal lines which resembled a modern capital I, which changed over time to the Z shape. *Zayin* is *zain* in Aramaic, and *zayn* in Syriac and Arabic.

*Zayin* also is the seventh letter of the Hebrew alphabet, and in biblical times meant "sword." The meanings of "weapon" and "sword" are interesting in light of how the Z-entities operate: they are weapons themselves that craftily calculate how to attack humans. Even more curious, *zayin* in modern Hebrew slang means "penis." Zozo is fond of sexual innuendoes and remarks.

In early Latin, Z was the seventh letter of the alphabet, not the last. Around 300 BCE, the Roman Censor Appius Claudius Caecus removed Z from the alphabet on the grounds that it was abhorrent and repulsive. Caecus disliked the sounding of the letter Z, which forced the lips to pull over the teeth, thus resembling a death-grin of a corpse.

After Rome conquered Greece in the first century BCE, Z was reintroduced into Latin, but only for the *zeta* sound in borrowed Greek terms, which some scholars felt sounded dull without the Z. The letter remained rather orphaned in Latin, appearing only in personal names and proper nouns.

Z was dropped from Early English and was replaced by S, but managed to survive on its own. It became common in medieval French, and made appearances in Germanic languages. The British still use S in place of Z when the letter falls within a word, and pronounce the letter by itself as "zed," a pronunciation borrowed from the Middle French *zede*, which in turn was derived from *zeta*. "Zed" mutated to "zee" in American English sometime in the eighteenth century, according to H.L. Mencken in his book *The American Language* (1919). Mencken did not speculate as to the reasons why.

Zed and Zee are not the only words for Z. In the mid-eighteenth century, the letter was called "izzard," a term that survived in secluded pockets of the United States well into the twentieth century. "Izzard" was used primarily as part of the expression "from A to Izzard," meaning anything that is all-inclusive.

## Dark characteristics of Z

Over the centuries, the unwanted letter Z has acquired dark superstitions and associations. As noted earlier, S has been used in place of Z in many spellings. Z and S are approximate mirror images of one another, which has given rise to folklore that Z, being the unwanted stepchild of the alphabet, is the evil twin of S.

Z has also been called the letter of uncertainty, prophecy, and eschatology (theology concerned with death), judgment, and the final destiny of the soul and of humankind.

It is the "weaponized" letter, due to its Phoenician associations, and thus is the letter of mutilation. The zig zag of the Z, like a razor blade, cuts and slashes. It is the dramatic mark of Zorro, a fictional character who has Zozo-like characteristics of remaining masked and unknown, and operating in a crafty, stealthy, and fox-like manner.

When pronounced in an extended manner, like zzzzzzz, Z has a buzzing quality and energy. Buzzing sounds occur in transdimensional shifts, such as when entities break through to the physical reality. In some cases of negative hauntings, attachments, and possession, there are hordes of buzzing and stinging insects that manifest. Zzzzzz sounds like an electrical charge, or the zzzt! when a bug flies into a zapper. Z words are often high voltage words such as zap, zing, zoom, zip, zig zag, zest, and zowie.

In short, Z carries a mystery and energy not found in other letters of the alphabet.

At the opposite end of the energy scale, Z is also connected to emptiness, dead ends, zero, zilch, zoned out, zonked, and the soulless zombie. At this end, the extended zzzzz relates to sleep and being "dead to the world."

One of the most stinging condemnations of Z was penned by Roland Barthes, a French literary theorist. In his work S/Z, (1970), a critique of author Honore de Balzac's short story, "Sarrazine,"

Barthes addresses Balzac's use of the z in spelling "Sarrazine" instead of "Sarrasin":

> Z is the letter of mutilation: phonetically, Z stings like a chastising lash, an avenging insect; graphically, cast slantwise by the hand across the blank regularity of the page, amid the curves of the alphabet, like an oblique and illicit blade, it cuts, slashes, or, as we say in French, *zebras*; from a Balzacian viewpoint, this Z (which appears in Balzac's name) is the letter of deviation.

No wonder the Z-entities are attracted to the letter Z. It is rare in usage, misunderstood, unappreciated, isolated, strange, and out of the ordinary.

## Missing letter Z

A strange oversight happened when the popular television series *Supernatural* licensed an official Hasbro, Inc. Ouija board. Purchasers were surprised when they opened up the box to find that the board was missing the letter Z. A spokesperson said it was a design matter—the board had copied the version used on the show, which also had no Z. There was clearly enough room to fit a Z on the surface, however. Despite the official explanation, rumors circulated that the Z was purposely left out in an attempt to thwart encounters with Zozo. Whatever the reason, the missing Z adds to the mystery to of the Zozo Phenomenon.

## Alien connections

Have the Z-entities invaded our communication with extraterrestrials? We find strange links between aliens and spirit boards in the case of a famous contactee in the 1950s, George Hunt Williamson. He is credited with helping usher in a deeper understanding of UFOs. His familiarity with Native American lore convinced him that similar alien contact stories existed all over the world. Williamson made headlines by his claims of making contact with alien intelligences through automatic writing, telepathy, ham radio, and spirit boards.

Born in Chicago in 1936, Williamson had an early interest in the occult and paranormal, fueled in part by an out-of-body experience he had as a teen. The post-World War II contact literature involving advanced alien intelligences and "space brothers" ignited his curiosity in the UFO field. In 1951, he picked up a copy of Donald Keyhoe's now-classic work, *The Flying Saucers Are Real* (1950), and gobbled it up in a single sitting. He also discovered the work of one of the most famous contactees of all, George Adamski, and joined his cult of followers.

In 1952, Williamson and his wife, Betty, were visited in their Tucson, Arizona home by two friends, Alfred and Betty Bailey, who shared their ET and occult interests. They amused themselves by trying to contact aliens via automatic writing, and received a message from an ET who said he was aboard a spaceship.

The four continued with automatic writing and then advanced to a home-made spirit board to establish more detailed communication with the unseen visitors. One of the board communications was as follows:

> Good and evil forces are working now. Organization is important for the salvation of your world. Contact us as soon as you can. There is a mass of planets in the organization. Why are your peoples [sic] unbelievers? You have begun the research. The time is up to you! Look up into the skies above you. We are friends of those interested, but we are not interested in those of carnal mind. By that we mean the stupid preservation of self; disregarding the will of the Creative Spirit and His Sons.

After communicating over the spirit board in several other messages, the aliens suggested a more efficient means of communication: radio. Williamson and Bailey complied and began using a ham radio, though they still used a spirit board as well. The radio yielded coded signals similar to Morse code but difficult to understand.

The aliens gave warnings of events that proved true, and so Williamson and Bailey grew confident of the reliability and trustworthiness of the aliens. (This is a common phenomenon in trickster board contact, where the initials communications are friendly and accurate, but soon followed by darker warnings and even threats.)

One of the principal communicators was Zo, who said he was leader of a group on Mars (called Masar), but was originally from Neptune. Zo and the other aliens referred to Earth as Saras, and delivered dire warnings of destruction at the hands of evil planetary men in cahoots with evil people on Saras. Also, evil beings from Orion were planning mass landings in order to conquer Saras. Zo—who professed to be one of the good aliens—instructed the men to prepare for transmissions from the alien group in Morse code, an event that allegedly was accompanied by strange lights over Winslow, Arizona, where the Baileys lived.

The aliens even promised a landing for a face-to-face meeting and gave an exact date and time. Elated, the Williamsons and Baileys packed up a lunch and set off in two cars. Somehow, they got separated and lost, and missed the appointment—a "chance of a lifetime," lamented Williamson.

The messages continued, transmitted vis spirit board, ham radio, and also telepathy. Williamson became convinced that mass landings were imminent.

Meanwhile, the Williamsons and Baileys became close with Adamski, who was getting his own dire warnings of landings and disaster. George and Alfred were among a small group that Adamski took into the California desert in November 1952 for a personal meeting with an alien, a Venusian named Orthon. The "meeting" consisted of Adamski walking alone some distance and over a hill, and then coming back to report on his meeting. Nonetheless, Williamson backed up Adamski, claiming that a great meeting of telepathic contact had taken place. The incident changed the dynamics of the personal relationships, however, with Adamski withdrawing and becoming more secretive. Williamson and Bailey went their own way.

In 1954, Williamson and Bailey published an account of their personal communications with Zo and company in a book, *The Saucers Speak!* Williamson went on to write several other books.

None of the apocalyptic warnings bore out, similar to the dire warnings that are often given in trickster spirit board communications.

Williamson remained a popular contactee throughout the 1950s. He stated that governments and "secret world rulers" would never provide disclosure of contact with extraterrestrials.

In 1959, he dropped out of the public eye. He changed his name to Michael d'Obrenovic, his supposed real name, because his UFO interests were damaging his career in anthropology. Little was heard from him after that, and he died in 1986.

Ufologist Nick Redfern later uncovered evidence that Williamson had been a "person of interest" to the FBI, in part because he claimed that the aliens had given him technology that could bring down U.S. military aircraft from the skies.

The alien messages of Williamson and other contactees remain as puzzling as many spirit board messages. Some of them ring true, some do not, and in between is a gray muddle of trickster material.

## An alien harlot queen?

In 1939, a woman named Dana Howard, who lived near the highly haunted Superstition Mountains in Arizona, said she was abducted straight off her living room couch by aliens from Venus, who also took a Native American and a prospector. Her abduction so affected her life that she authored about eight books detailing her arduous abduction to the planet Venus. Howard described living among Venusians, who were ruled by "Queen Zo-na."

Perhaps even stranger than the tale itself is that "zona" in Hebrew is "whore" or "bitch." The insult "ben zona" means "son of a bitch" or "whore's son."

## Z and Martians

Ever since the polar ice caps of Mars were discovered by telescope in the mid-seventeenth century, humans have speculated on the existence of life on the red planet. This interest has intensified since the late twentieth century with our ability to send probes to Mars for close-up photographs. The famous "face on Mars" at an area called Cydonia was first imaged by the Viking 1 orbiter in July, 1976. In photographs taken subsequently by other probes, people have reported seeing markings and formations that resemble the letters Y and Z in features on the surface of the planet. Sometimes the Y shape is alone, and sometimes accompanied by the Z. If the Z is present, it is usually below the Y.

In his UFO news report, *Filer's Files #12*, March 22, 2006, George Filer commented on a photograph of the depression of Juventae Chasma in the plains of Lunae Planum taken in March 2004 by the High Resolution Stereo Camera (HRSC) on board the European Space Agency's Mars Express spacecraft. Said Filer:

> We know that the letter or symbol "Y" is often found on rocks and what appear to be signs on Mars. I speculate that writing was carved on each side of the large mine. Later these symbols were brought to Earth by aliens who used the symbols Y and Z.
>
> There is a mountain composed of bright, layered material that appears to be an open pit mine. This mountain is approximately 2500 metres high, 59 kilometres long and up to 23 kilometres wide. At each end of the mountain is writing or symbols that appear to start with the symbol "Y." The sign is several miles wide...
>
> The letter "Y" is now used on Earth by 32 different languages. The legends of many nations such as Egypt claim aliens or gods brought writing to Earth. The ancient Egyptians called their writing "words of god," a gift from Thoth, the ibis headed god of learning and writing.
>
> The "Y" was used in ancient Egyptian writing at the ruins of the Temple of Amun-Re. This is the largest columnar structure ever built... in the sacred lake at Karnak. The temples cover a square mile...
>
> ...Carved into some of the largest columns in the world we have found the letters "Y" and "Z." These columns are 52 feet high and were built in 2400 BC. I believe this is more than a coincidence.

Were the letters Y and Z brought to Earth by aliens? If so, what was their original meaning?

## Z aerial anomalies

Organizations that collect reports of UFOs often receive reports of mysterious lights, clouds, mists, and other aerial phenomena—and sometimes the letter Z is involved.

On the night of the full moon on July 10, 1998, a huge Z-shaped light illuminated the skies on both sides of the Irish Sea. Dozens of eyewitnesses phoned in reports. The Z was described as being as big in apparent size in the sky as the full moon. It lingered in the sky for more than an hour and floated slowly westward. It was higher than clouds, which sometimes obscured it. Sightings were centered in northern Ireland, but extended to Cornwall and Leeds in England, and into Scotland.

Authorities said a meteor that broke up in the atmosphere was responsible—despite the fact that meteor trails disappear quickly and do not last for more than an hour.

A Z-shaped cloud was reported to the Mutual UFO Network on May 17, 2015 by an eyewitness in Ottawa, Ontario, Canada. The witness was using binoculars to look at a strange "cloud" that did not appear to be a real cloud, but perhaps a solid object with a tail. A jet passed close to it, and then the "cloud" took on the form of a letter Z. The eyewitness said:

> Then after the plane disappeared from site to the west I realized that the "cloud" had formed the letter Z in the sky, which means it went in those directions to form that letter. And not only that, but I was stunned when the Z plainly stayed in the same position in the sky in the west for over 3/4 of an hour. I have never seen a formation of clouds lasting more than a couple of minutes, if that, but this pattern was sticking. Very strange indeed...
>
> ...At first I thought the object was the trail of a jet but the trail was way too thick for that, as the front was moving in a slow but deliberate path and the front was more solid, as I said. When I first saw the object, I was still thinking it might be a plane trail or just an odd cloud, but couldn't take my eyes off it. It was then I realized it was moving and not like a cloud, but like the tail was being led by the oval solid object at the front of it—attached it seemed.

If Z is a letter that originated with aliens, then might these aerial Z shapes be a code, such as an activation code? The mystery of Z deepens.

## Zozo oddities

The dark nature of the letter Z carries over into "zozo" words and names. The term "zozo" and its shortened version "zo" have many associations with the unpleasant, the dark, the dangerous, the demonic, the depressed, the powerful, the promiscuous, and the defiled. We found various Zo and derivative words and names that made curious roundabout connections with the talking board Zozo.

In Voodoo, "zozo" is a term for "penis." Among the Zulu, "zozo" means "ulcer" or "natal sore," a spreading scourge forming on the feet and shins.

In Melanesia, it is a term for "walking spirit." The zozo spirit is believed to leave the body and bring back to the sleeper its contact with the dead.

In French, "zozo" is slang for "twit." The term is used for the proper name of the Devil in works by French playwright Jacques Audeberti (1899-1965). Audeberti was a supporter of the Theatre of the Absurd, a style of theater popular in the mid-twentieth century that dealt with themes such as the meaninglessness of human life and breakdown of communication. By literally labeling the Devil as a "twit," Audeberti held the Devil up to ridicule.

Zozo has even invaded children's books, appearing as an ugly "naughty alien monster" who "eats greedily" in *A Farewell for Yobi* (Utusan, 2005) by Loh Chung Tat. Yobi, the hero, is an alien scientist who battles Zozo and defeats him in a "push and pull challenge."

## Zozobra

*Zozobra* is a Spanish term meaning "gloomy one," "anxiety," or "anxious," all traits associated with the spirit board Zozo.

In particular, Zozobra ("Old Man Gloom") is the name of an effigy that is publicly burned every fall in Santa Fe, New Mexico, to kick off the Fiestas de Santa Fe. The ritual began in 1926 when artist Will Shuster introduced a six-foot Zozobra puppet to be set ablaze. Zozobra has grown to about fifty feet in height, and is made of muslin stuffed with sheets of paper. It looks like a grotesque, red-eyed ghost dressed in white and black. The purpose of burning Zozobra is to chase away gloom and depression. The puppet puts on quite a show, groaning and flailing about as it is consumed by flames. While it burns, dances of ghosts are performed.

Also burned is a box full of papers stating the gloomy and bad things that individuals want to banish. The box is placed at Zozobra's feet and burns along with him.

It is curious that Zozo and Zozobra share negativity—problems that weigh people down and deteriorate the quality of life.

## African connections

In West Africa, powerful secret societies such as the leopard, snake, and Poro are ruled by priests called *zoes* (singular *zo*). The *zoes* have great magical power over bush spirits, including those that possess people. Rituals of human sacrifice and cannibalism have been attributed to these secret societies. Such rituals are not uncommon throughout history in parts of the world, for blood sacrifice is considered to be the best appeasement of gods and spirits, and consuming flesh is a magical way of absorbing the traits and powers of the victims. The interesting connection here is *zo*, and, once again, the attributes of rulership and magical powers.

Another interesting association with Africa is found in *The Wide World Magazine*, a British monthly that was published from April 1898 to December 1965. Its motto was "Truth is stranger than fiction." The magazine ran "true-life" adventure and travel stories, some in installments, that were full of lurid descriptions and purple prose. The magazine was exposed for fraud for publishing an elaborate hoax about a white man's adventures in the Australian bush, although it is not clear whether or not the author perpetrated the hoax upon the magazine. Hoax journalist was rampant in the late nineteenth to early twentieth centuries, as newspapers and magazines competed for readers, as we have noted previously. Stories of wild adventures and attacks by monstrous creatures were common.

True or not, a story published in the magazine in 1901 has interesting associations with the term "zozo." The article describes a trip through "a province called Zozo" in Africa. "Zozo" eventually became Zazzau and then Zaria, a city in northern Nigeria. The various clans in Zozo were once ruled by kings.

The author of the article describes the Zozo province as:

> ...abutted on several other provinces, each of which vomited into it its rogues and vagabonds, to fight among themselves, to fight each other, and to kill, torture, burn, and enslave the members of the multinudinous small Pagan tribes that inhabited it.
>
> When we passed through this little scrap of Nature, it was a regular pandemonium. It was overrun by bank robbers, scoured by slave raiders, oppressed by troops that professed to police it, and torn to pieces by bursts of fury on the part of the rankly savage native tribes who claimed it as their own, and who, individually and collectively, behaved sometimes like scared beasts and at others like mad demons.
>
> In addition to this, the countryside was haunted by solitary, ghoul-like individuals, who seemed to have no object save rapine and murder...

Once again, we are struck by the extreme negative associations with the word or name Zozo, and by the connection to kingship, which is a boast that Zozo likes to make. We stress that there is no direct link to the spirit board Zozo entity, but the common ground shared by all of these associations is dark, gloomy, and violent.

## The OZ/ZO Synchronicity

Perhaps all of these weird connections form a peculiar type of synchronicity. Jake Kotz is a writer popular among conspiracy theorist circles, and has noticed a strange connection with Oz and Zo in what he describes as "synchromysticism." Kotz coined that term in 2006 and defines it as "the art of realizing meaningful coincidence in the seemingly mundane with mystical or esoteric significance."

In his blog called "Rant in Z minor," Kotz attributes the words Oz and Zo as *resonators* that show up in various media such as comic books, television, and movies. He draws parallels between the words Oz and Zo and provides examples of how these words link to various media and Aleister Crowley, such as in his book *Liber Oz/77*. The article mentions Jungian psychology, Gnosticism, and the Jimmy Page Zoso symbol. In correspondence with Darren, Kotz relayed that any significance to the word Zozo, might be found within this "synchromystic" field of study.

One of those synchomysticism connections can be found in *The Wonderful Wizard of Oz* (1900), a children's novel by L. Frank Baum and immortalized in 1939 in the film *The Wizard of Oz* starring Judy Garland. The story follows the adventures of young Dorothy, who, with her dog Toto, is swept up by a tornado and deposited in the magical Land of Oz. She is informed by the Good Witch that the only way she can get back home to Kansas is to find the all-powerful, terrifying Wizard of Oz and appeal for his help. After many adventures, Dorothy discovers that Oz, who is hidden behind a curtain, is only a "humbug"— an ordinary man with no special powers who has managed to pull off a fraud. All ends well for Dorothy and her travelling companions, the Cowardly Lion, the Tin Man, and the Scarecrow. The wizard exits Oz by the same way he arrived, via a hot air balloon.

Many allegorical associations have been made to the story, and we can add some ones of our own. The Djinn are associated with whirlwinds, and so Dorothy, like the unsuspecting spirit board user, is whisked by the Djinn into an alternate reality fraught with pitfalls and dangers. The all-powerful Wizard of Oz (Zozo) strikes fear into others, but is revealed in the end to be powerless in his own right—the only power he has is what is conferred on him by the fear of others. He is, like his mode of transport, nothing but "hot air." He does, however, make Dorothy's companions realize that what they want, they have all along—all they have to do is take their own power.

Zozo is able to terrify spirit board users via an illusion of power and the "hot air" of intimidation.

An even stranger footnote to Oz is the Pink Floyd connection: their album *The Dark Side of the Moon* (1973), when synchronized with the beginning of the 1939 film, matches the action of the film in a weird, surrealistic way. The moon is a symbol of illusion, and the dark side is the unknown and uncertain.

When it comes to Oz/Zozo, we are floating in a sea of illusion.

## The blackbird connection

In the Basque language, "zozo" means "crow" or "blackbird." Black birds in general are messengers from the spirit world. Crows and ravens are found on many talking boards designs, probably because of their associations with magic and prophecy. Darren, as mentioned earlier, found preserved dead blackbirds with the original Zozo board, and had an unexplained supernatural experience with ravens while filming *I Am Zozo*.

Every animal and bird has its positive and negative associations in lore, but all types of black birds fall more on the dark side than most other birds. They are tricksters, thieves, shapeshifters, spies, tattlers, and omens of death, pestilence, ill health, and disaster.

The Norse god Odin keeps a pair of raven spies, which he sends out every morning to make note of everything going on around the world. The birds even talk to the dead. Odin himself has the ability to shapeshift into a raven.

In fairy lore, fairies shapeshift into crows when they make mischief. The Devil is said to favor black forms, such as black birds and black dogs.

In Irish lore, the triple goddess known as The Morrigan, represented by Macha, Babd, and Nemain (who is sometimes replaced by Anand), take the forms of crows and ravens. They fly over battlefields to instigate fighting, and pluck the souls of the slain.

Crows and ravens eat carrion, and, according to lore, can smell the scent of death upon a person before they die, even through the walls of a house. They pluck out the eyes of sinners, and especially like the corpses of hanged criminals.

In the Bible, the raven is considered an "unclean" bird, along with the owl. In Christian lore, ravens symbolize the sins of gluttony, theft, and false teaching, and carry off the souls of the damned. It was once believed that evil priests became ravens when they died.

The song of the blackbird (a type of thrush) is associated with sexual temptation. According to lore, the Devil, in the form of a blackbird, flew into the face of St. Benedict in order to stir within him sexual desire. The saint tore off his clothes and jumped into a thorn bush in order to quench the desire, and reportedly he was never troubled by lust again.

All of these negative associations are significant when applied to the behavior of the talking board Zozo, who is deceitful, often delivers prophetic messages of death, makes threats of killing, expresses lust, indicates that it watches and spies on people, and seems to shapeshift from one alter ego to another, even into masquerades of the dead.

Darren is not the only board user to experience a connection between the board and ravens. Here is an example from an experiencer:

> I had an experience a year ago, where my younger sister brought a board to my house. It was a glow in the dark Ouija board, and it would only produce movement for me and my sister. We tried several variations of people. The planchette spun irrationally around the board, between the letters M and A, for about an hour. I didn't put together until after the situation that it could have meant MAMA. It spelled it over and over and wouldn't spell any other word except MAYBE once. My sister said she heard it say that in her head.
>
> My sister also told me she saw a raven shortly after she bought the board. I am "sensitive" and see things, I have seen a demon my whole life and I have reason to believe this "mama" could be what I've seen? I've also seen a different entity lately.
>
> I am debating trying to build my own spirit board to try to communicate successfully. I used the Ouija that one time and I still feel the presence around me. I'd rather face it than fear it.

There is another significant blackbird connection to Zozo. In lore, the eerie song of the blackbird can put listeners into a trance-like state. Jimmy Page, the lead guitarist of Led Zeppelin, joined a band called The Black Crows after his Led Zeppelin fame. Page also had used his "Zoso" symbol with The Black Crows on the cover of *Live at the Greek*. After the breakup of Led Zeppelin, Page wanted to plan a reunion tour and recruited singer Myles Kennedy, who joined forces with X Creed band members to front the group Alterbridge. The band's second effort was simply called *Blackbird*.

## Zozo the soul stealer

In 1926, Zozo made headlines in the New York City newspapers—but not as a spirit. "Zozo" was the stage name of an astrologer and palm reader who was popular with wealthy patrons. What makes the case bizarre is that the human Zozo acted just like the later talking board Zozo, mesmerizing people and allegedly putting them under spells. His wife accused him of controlling her in her dreams, and even stealing her soul.

During the 1920s, many stories of Ouija-related strange behavior surfaced in the media, which Rosemary documents in her book co-authored with Rick Fisher, *Ouija Gone Wild* (2012). There were so many cases of people acting out in weird ways on the advice of board spirits that the media called it "Ouija Mania," and cases erupted all over the country for nearly a decade.

The Ouija board was only a few decades old at that point, and was just coming into its first rush of popularity. Most people looked upon the spirit board as entertainment, but some consulted it for serious advice.

We wonder now: were tricky board spirits such as Zozo trying out their wings then, to see how people could be influenced? We also wonder about the palmist named Zozo. Where did he come up with the name? No spirit board is mentioned in the articles about the man Zozo. Was the name implanted by an entity who influenced him to mimic the entity's behavior? Or did the talking board Zozo copy the palmist? Since we have found historical evidence of a possessing demon named Zozo, perhaps it is the former. Zozo the man was an American, and maintained several residences, including one in France—but would he have adopted a slang term for "twit" as his professional name? It seems unlikely.

Here is the story from a New York City newspaper, the headline of which reads **"Claims 'Zozo' Her Svengali"**:

Here is a woman whose complaint falls with the confines of no man-made law. Hence, no court has authorization to pass upon it. The woman claims her former husband steals her soul.

Mrs. Laura Broosk Ellwanger Kenilworth, former wife of "Zozo," who for years enjoyed extensive patronage as a society seer among the "sets" of Manhattan, Newport, and Atlantic City, made this amazing charge. She declared Walter Winston Kenilworth ("Zozo"), the stargazer and reader of wealthy palms, committed the theft of a wife's soul and in return projected "part" of his own personality onto the wife's spiritual being.

She has spent a large personal fortune, she declared yesterday, in dispensing fees to world-famous mental analysts, psychologists and neurologists in a fruitless campaign in quest of her "stolen" soul. Only a few months ago she submitted to hypnotic treatment at the hands of a noted mesmerist, endeavoring to respond to the suggestions that her soul had been returned.

## Where is her soul?

Characterizing herself as broken in health and spirit, she narrated her psychic history in an interview at an uptown hotel where she maintains a suite. The woman's story rivals in its aspects the fictional mental processes attributed to the dual personality character in Stevenson's "Dr. Jekyll and Mr. Hyde," and compares in its incongruities to the psychic control exercised by Svengali over Trilby.

She said:

"My former husband, 'Zozo,' sailed a few weeks ago for France, where he has a luxurious villa. My soul went with him. Again and again I have pleaded with him to return that which he stole—my astral spirit. He even stole my dreams and so controls my actions that I never dream except at his command, and then only to see a vision of him commanding me to do his weird dictates.

"I am forty-two years old. Kenilworth is forty-five, large and handsome. I was married to him November 21, 1918. We were husband and wife for a year and eight months. Immediately after the ceremony he announced his intention of dominating me completely. He would sit every day at a stated time and concentrate on this unusual thing. It took him seven months to accomplish the theft of my soul. From then until now life has held nothing in store for me.

## Soul Soars Meantime

"I procured a divorce on the ground of cruelty, for what is more cruel than the theft of a woman's soul. Of course it would have appeared ridiculous to a court to say that my soul had been stolen, so I took other examples of his mental cruelty for my action. Kenilworth was known in private life as Walter K. Martin. He had an establishment at Atlantic City, and others at Newport, in New York city, and in Paris.

"He is a man of dominant willpower and has a magnetic personality that causes people to fall at his feet when he so wills it. He held the palms of rich old ladies and read from them, apparently, for the rich old ladies wouldn't understand Kenilworth if he told them he was peering into their astral spirits. Thus humoring them, his income was not less than $100 a day, and many of the rich old ladies have been eager to hurl their fortunes and their love at him.

"Yet, as much money as he made and as many opportunities as he must have had to dupe these doting old ladies of fashion and wealth, I never knew him to take a penny diabolically. All he wanted was to steal souls, not money.

## Vulgar to Steal Money

"He said that was vulgar.

"When I asked him by what right he stole my soul, he answered:

"'There, there, my dear! I am doing it by right of intellect. You have a suburban intellect. I am a genius.'"

"Shortly after our marriage (I was his second wife, his first having been a wealthy Boston woman sixty-six years old, from whom he separated after one year's 'bliss' and whose fortune of $100,000 was left him on her death) I dreamed that 'Zozo' pushed me forcibly in a body of water and explained:

"'I do not want your worldly goods, but you must die.'"

"In this vision, one of the last of my prophetic dreams, I fought with all my spirit's strength to be saved, but finally I lost.

"Two weeks later, after my dream my hair, which had always been very thick, began to fall out and my mental force grew somewhat feeble. All the months that followed the vision was [sic] spent away from my husband, he living in one city and I in another, but his psychic force was dominating me all the while.

"Doctoring, I still held the firm conviction that my astral nature was gone because I no longer had visions. Kenilworth, in a gust of anger one day when I returned to plead for my soul remarked:

'I have dominated you, you will never come back.'

## Look At Him Now:

"Now, as to the other person as it worked in Kenilworth's own body. In September, 1919, it was Kenilworth, who was coming back.

"What a change!

"Before me stood a boyish man with the exact duplicate of my own features chiseled upon his own. Contrawise, my own features were beginning to grow like his, and my voice was almost like his!

"Whereas before I had been a total abstainer and Kenilworth had 'hit the booze strong,' as the saying is, the reverse was true. I had intense cravings for alcohol, so much so that I had to seek medical advice. On the other hand, Kenilworth was entirely sober and cared nothing for his whiskey. When I married him he was in his middle forties. In September, 1919, he seemed a rejuvenated man. Formerly he had been severe looking, without a vestige of youthfulness in manner or countenance. I had been transformed into a hopeless wreck from a gently, sympathetic, and sprightly girl-woman.

"One famous diagnostic of New York, whom I was obliged to consult, gave me his opinion that it was a projection of a strong will upon a weaker one. Kenilworth for years had studied the laws of cosmos and psychic control. I was, indeed, his Trilby, and he was my Svengali. From 116 pounds in weight, I have fallen off to ninety-five pounds.

## Landlords Under Spell

"On several occasions I have gone to an apartment at Kenilworth's psychic command, rented it, and paid deposits. The very next day, under the control of that man's sinister mind, I would leave my deposits, go and take up a room or suite in a hotel. One day I had a consuming desire for oranges. I ate eighteen of them. Later I heard Kenilworth laughingly remark that he had been standing at the orange dealer's near his Atlantic City establishment and merely had exercised his control vanity.

"At that time I was in Philadelphia, which shows the sheer force of his will. He has made me suspicious of my relatives and friends, and I often suffer a delusion that food served me had been poisoned.

"My last vision, commanded by Kenilworth, showed me the man embarking for Europe. Across his breast was a placard, which read:

"Commit suicide."

The spirit board Zozo could not have done better himself.

# 14

## The Power of Zozo's Name

Zozo boasts that its secret power that enables it to manifest to so many people is in its name—which is no surprise, considering the characteristics of the letter Z. The more people who speak Zozo's name and enable it to spell its name out on a board, the more power the entity acquires in any given environment. In certain cases, if conditions are right, it acquires enough power to latch on to a person or place, enabling it to invade dreams, pester someone mentally, and create unpleasant poltergeist disturbances. Zozo can do the same when it manifests on other kinds of spirit communication tools and methods, such as ghost boxes, pendulums, and automatic writing.

Merely saying the name of an entity, or reading about it, is not going to automatically summon it to your presence, however. Many spirit board users do not even know who Zozo is until after the fact. As Zozo has become better known, its name does evoke reactions in people, from curiosity to fear. A collective focus on Zozo lends it strength and energy.

There are some interesting links between Zozo and its alternate names and magic.

## Magical names and words

The power of a name to summon is well known in magical practices that have been developed since ancient times. A name is a vibration of energy. In magical invocations and evocations, names and words of power are "vibrated," that is, spoken with such great force and authority that the vibration of the sound is felt through the entire body. This is done with the accompanying understanding of what the name or word means, and an intense projection of energy and will toward a desired result.

The magical power of names and words has been recognized since antiquity. All cultures have used them in their magical rituals, for names embody the identity of a person or being and convey and determine personality, power, essence, qualities, luck, destiny and fate.

The ancient civilizations of Babylonia, Assyria, and Egypt ascribed great importance to the power of names for invoking and commanding spirits. Amulets with sacred names were worn to ward off demonic forces and the evil eye.

Names were especially important in Egyptian religious and magical practice. God names had creative power. According to the story of creation, in the beginning the gods were not born, but came into being by uttering a name. The god Osiris first formed a mouth. According to the Papyrus of Nesi-Amsu, Osiris stated, "I brought [fashioned] my mouth, and I uttered my own name as a word of power, and thus I evolved myself..."

The Egyptians believed that a person's personal name was an integral part of him, as important as his *ka* or soul, and thus also had magical power. The tombs of kings and royalty were inscribed with god names in the belief that as those names would be preserved, energized and empowered, so would the name of the dead person, and thus his soul would prosper as well.

The Egyptian *Book of the Dead* emphasizes the importance of names in the underworld journey of the deceased. In one part of the underworld kingdom of Osiris are seven halls or mansions, each guarded by a doorkeeper, a watcher and a herald. The deceased must know the correct names of all the guardians in order to pass through all halls. Success meant having freedom of movement and access through all seven Halls of Osiris. Many other passages in the underworld journey had to be navigated by using correct names.

In magical rituals, names were invoked with great precision and accurate pronunciation; anything less meant failure. Many gods and lesser spirits had *numerous names and forms*, any and all of which might be invoked in order to cover all bases. Wax figures of gods were inscribed with names, and whatever was done to the figure was done to the god—a form of sympathetic magic.

In the Western magical tradition, names of power had acquired great importance by medieval times. The correct use of them was transmitted orally to initiates, and also in magical texts known as grimoires. In Jewish mysticism, names of power were both disguised and created by the systems of *gematria*, *notarikon* and *temurah*, which calculated numerical values of the Hebrew letters. Words that shared the same numerical values acquired significance. In coded texts, words with the same numerical value could be substituted as blinds.

Grimoires flourished in Europe in the seventeenth to nineteenth centuries, culminating in the secret teachings of the Hermetic Order of the Golden Dawn, an esoteric order founded in 1889 in London. Though not intended to be a magical lodge, the Golden Dawn became one, attracting all the intellectual and magical personalities of the day—including Aleister Crowley. In the magic of Crowley, we find interesting connections to Zozo.

First we have to go back in time a few centuries to the "angel" communications of John Dee and Edward Kelly. We have put *angel* in quotations marks, because the actual identities of the beings Dee and Kelly contacted is uncertain.

## Enochian magic

John Dee (1527-1608) was an alchemist, mathematician, astronomer, and astrologer, sometimes called "the last royal magician" because of his astrological services to Queen Elizabeth I. He was one of the most learned men in Europe, and he was fascinated by the occult and magic. He devoted most of his life to trying to communicate with spirits, for which he had to rely on mediums due to his own lack of psychic ability. To a man, his partners were all scalawags and con artists, including his most famous partner of all, Edward Kelly.

At the time, the quest for gold via alchemy was all the rage in Europe. Alchemists labored away in their secret rooms trying to find the magical means of transmuting base metals such as lead into silver or gold. The belief that this could be done was based on an esoteric principle that all things eventually evolve to their perfect forms, even over millions of years. Alchemy could speed things along.

Dee had money problems and thought alchemy could bail him out. He paid attention to his dreams and tried to contact spirits for help via scrying, which is gazing into a shiny surface such as a stone or crystal. Dee had a crystal egg that he called the "shew-stone," and a black obsidian mirror. His lack of success prompted him to find a mediumistic partner. When he met Edward Kelly in 1582, he thought he had struck gold.

Dee and Kelly never achieved any alchemical success. Instead, Kelly contacted what he said were angels, who started giving instructions for ushering in a new aeon of spirituality. This appealed to Dee, who already considered himself to be a messiah for Judgment Day, which he believed to be on the horizon. The angels dictated elaborate magical square formulas, and communicated in a language called Enochian, which Kelly could understand and would translate for Dee. They also gave alchemical advice—which never led to success.

In the beginning, the archangels Michael, Gabriel, Raphael, and Uriel made their appearances, but they soon gave way to more frequent appearances by angels with names not previously known. These spirits were parts of families. One had the appearance of a young woman who, on at least one occasion, appeared in the nude to Kelly.

Over time, Dee and Kelly developed a series of nineteen "calls" or keys for evoking the "angels." The calls enabled an ascension of consciousness through levels called aethyrs.

Most of Dee's diaries did not survive, but enough of them did to pass on into later magical lore. The calls were incorporated into a system of Enochian magic, which was of importance to the Hermetic Order of the Golden Dawn.

Enter Aleister Crowley (1875-1947), a talented, flamboyant, and precocious man renowned for his magical talents at an early age. He, too, saw himself as the prophet of a New Aeon of spirituality, one that would supplant all other religions. Crowley was initiated into the Golden Dawn in 1898. His time there was short and fiery.

The Enochian Keys were studied at length by Crowley, who explored all of them and pronounced them genuine. In his biography and autobiography, *The Confessions of Aleister Crowley* (1969), he states that "...anyone with the smallest capacity for Magick finds that they work." (Crowley spelled "magic" with a k to distinguish real magic from stage magic.) Even beginners in magic get results with Enochian calls, he said. Crowley's most extensive commentary on the magic of the Keys was published in his book *The Vision and the Voice* in 1911.

Despite the importance given the Keys by the Golden Dawn, which taught them to all adepts, there is no evidence that anyone but Crowley ever actually worked with them much; they were appreciated in theory but not in practice.

Crowley set out to accomplish all of the Enochian Keys. To do this, he would select a secluded spot and recite a Key to gain access to an aethyr. He would then gaze into a large golden topaz—his own version of Kelly's "shew-stone"—to scry for contact with spirits and astral beings.

In 1909, Crowley had a spectacular encounter with a demon named Choronzon during an Enochian ritual in the desert beyond Algiers with his assistant Victor Neuberg. Choronzon, also known as 333, the "Demon of the Abyss," and "Lord of Hallucinations," is one of the most feared entities in Enochian magic. It is the spirit of dissolution, undoing everything it touches, including the minds of human beings. It rules the Abyss, a chaos that has no center. It is considered to be quite dangerous and crafty. Choronzon is located in the Tenth Aethyr.

Crowley prepared for a ritual in which he would attempt to master Choronzon. According to the story, Choronzon breached the magical boundaries of the circle that protected Neuberg and wrestled physically with him, shapeshifting into various forms. Crowley was temporarily possessed by the demon—and some say he was forever affected by the experience.

When Crowley made the Call of the Tenth Aethyr, Choronzon announced himself from within the topaz with this cry: *Zazas, Zazas, Nasatanada Zazas,* and went on to say, "I am I...From me come leprosy and pox and plague and cancer and cholera and the falling sickness...”

Neuberg asserted that Crowley remained hooded and silent, and that the words issued from the shew-stone, However, it is likely that the entranced Crowley spoke them, serving as a conduit for the demon.

After the ritual was concluded, Crowley said that he felt he had identified completely with Choronzon, and both men said they understood the nature of the Abyss.

*Zazas, Zazas, Nasatanada Zazas* has since been used by many who attempt to invoke Choronzon. “Zazas” is striking similar to Zaza, the most common alter of Zozo. Might Zozo be an aspect of Choronzon? Zozo is crafty and cunning. Some persons who come into contact with the board entity suffer a dissolution, whether it be a mental breakdown or a deterioration in the peace and harmony of home.

There is a widely held view that Crowley opened up some powerful interdimensional portals with his magical work that enabled entities like Choronzon to access the physical realm, and without the necessity of ritual magic. The entity Lam, who has been compared to extraterrestrials, is another evoked by Crowley. What other entities have come through the portals?

Here is another interesting note to the Crowley connection: When his second daughter was born in 1906 to his first wife, Rose, Crowley named her Lola Zaza.

Rosemary has proposed that Crowley and Dee were dealing with Djinn. Demon or Djinn, the links back to Zozo are intriguing.

## The power of projection

Perhaps the greatest power of Zozo’s name lies not in ritual magic, but in the mind of the person using a spirit board, as we discussed earlier. Thrill-seekers—especially young people—openly or secretly hope for contact with a scary entity. For more than a decade, Zozo has grabbed most of the fear headlines related to spirit boards. In addition, board users who harbor any kind of anxiety (“What if I use a board and something bad happens?”) likewise are going to project an energy that will magnetize whatever they fear.

And, if a person is going to have a negative board experience that is worthy of reporting to others, it should be with the most dangerous entity of them all. Zozo's name reigns supreme—lesser tricksters and demonic entities need not respond.

Thus, Zozo is absolutely right in claiming that the power of its name enables it to manifest. The name has acquired power because people using the board have given it power. As we have discussed previously, Zozo has, in some respects, become a collective thoughtform, energized by untold numbers of board users, many of whom unwittingly send out a call whenever they put their fingers on a planchette.

"When we focus on something we give it a lot of power," said Robert Murch. "Zozo is more than just an entity. Zozo is the ultimate fear of playing with a spirit board. It's the worst story you can have, the worst case scenario. Zozo is extreme and dramatic."

The entity operating as Zozo is intelligent and quite a schemer. It has seized on a name that has all the trappings of fear: the lonesome Z with its strange sounds, and short, punchy names that immediately grab attention. A mysterious Z name, and especially one with a singsong repetition of sound, is bound to hook an audience.

# 15

## The Zoso Sigil

In 1971, Led Zeppelin released its fourth album, which was untitled. Signed on the inner sleeve were four symbols chosen by the four members of the band. Three of the symbols were familiar from esoteric lore, but the fourth, created by lead guitarist Jimmy Page, was a mystery. It was "the Zoso symbol."

Page said little about the symbol, other than that it was derived from existing texts. Given that clue, plus his interest in occultism and the works of Aleister Crowley, Page's fans worldwide set off on a search for the meaning of the Zoso symbol.

To understand the importance of the symbol, we need to once again revisit Crowley and also his contemporary, artist Austin Osman Spare (1888-1956). Crowley became fascinated with the magical work of Spare. We mention him because of his access to forces that might conceivably express an entity such as Zozo, as well as his connection to Crowley, and his skill with sigils, which again relate back to Zozo.

## The power of sigils

Sigils are symbols that express occult forces, such as contained in a set of ideas, sacred names, and the numerical essences of angels, intelligences, spirits, and planets. The term "sigil" comes from the Latin *sigillum*, which means "seal."

A sigil itself does not call forth spirits, but serves as a physical focus through which the practitioner achieves a desired state of mind. Its primary purpose is to stimulate the imagination in accordance with the purpose of a ritual. A sigil is given energy via visualization, chanting, and intensity of will, and then is activated or "sent." The correct use of sigils is one of the factors that determine the success of the ritual.

Sigils can be likened to a form of shorthand that enables a practitioner to set in motion cosmic forces, or summon spirits into awareness and control them. Some sigils are created from the numbers in magic squares. They also can be symbols, astrological signs, runes, and even unique designs. They can contain the entire essence of a spell, or the magical properties of celestial forces, spirits, or deities.

## Spare's magic

Spare developed his own magical system based on will and sexual energy, and the use of sigils to direct the force of both in order to manifest a desire. He has been called the father of chaos magic. Spare had great disdain for Crowley; it was rumored that Crowley made sexual advances to him, which Spare found repugnant.

Spare's introduction to serious magic came in childhood, in a relationship he had with a mysterious old woman named Mrs. Paterson. She claimed to be a hereditary witch descended from a line of Salem witches who escaped execution during the witch trials in 1692—an unlikely claim, considering that the Salem incident was perpetrated by hysterical children, and there was no evidence of hereditary "lines of witches."

Regardless of the truth of her claim, Mrs. Paterson had a great ability to manifest her thoughts, a skill she passed on to Spare. She taught him how to visualize and evoke spirits and elementals and how to reify, or reinterpret, his dream imagery. Information was transmitted from her to him in dreams with the help of Mrs.

Paterson's familiar, Black Eagle. She also initiated Spare in a witches' sabbat, which he described as taking place in another dimension, where cities were constructed of an unearthly geometry.

Under further tutelage of Mrs. Paterson, Spare developed his own system of magic, called the Zos Kia Cultus. At its simplest, Zos is the entire human body and its range of consciousness in the world, and Kia is imagination, a faculty necessary for accessing alternate realities. Spare believed that the power of will is capable of fulfilling any deeply held desire. His formula, simpler than ceremonial magic, was in his unpublished grimoire or magical text, *The Book of the Living Word of Zos*. The formula called for creating sigils or talismans in an "alphabet of desire."

The process is this: The desire is written down in full. Repeating letters are crossed out and the remaining letters are combined into a sigil like a sort of monogram. The sigil is impressed upon the subconscious by staring at it. The original desire is then let go so that the "god within" can work undisturbed toward the desired end.

Spare's success with sigils was extraordinary, and even accomplished experts in the magical arts came to him for help. Gerald B. Gardner, the founder of Gardnerian Wicca, asked Spare for a sigil to help him in a magical war with Crowley's associate, Kenneth Grant.

In his art, Spare was best known for his atavisms, the reifying (reinterpreting) of primal forces from previous existences, drawn from the deepest layers of the human mind. This, too, was a product of his education from Mrs. Paterson. Spare's atavisms are combination of human and bestial forms; some look demonic. They are not evil per se, but expressions of powerful forces. It is conceivable that Zozo resides among atavisms.

## Led Zeppelin

Jimmy Page enjoyed incredible success as the soft spoken guitarist of the legendary rock group Led Zeppelin. For the band's fourth album, Page inspired the band members to choose symbols to represent their names on the album cover. Page chose the strange symbol "Zoso" and did not identify the occult reference texts that were its source. "Zoso" is not a word. Page said that the formation of something that can look like a word is purely coincidental. Was Zoso a sigil—something intended for making contact with the spirit world?

Page was at one time deeply fascinated with the occult and acquired the largest collection of the artwork and writings of Aleister Crowley. He opened an occult bookstore called The Equinox, where he traded and sold in rare books and occult artifacts.

In 1970, Page purchased Crowley's former residence located on the Scotland shores of Loch Ness, Boleskine House, where Crowley performed complicated magical workings, and spread his floor with river sand in order to detect the presence of spirits. Crowley bought the house in 1899 because he considered it an ideal, remote place in which to perform magic from the grimoire The Book of Abramelin, supposedly magic taught from an Egyptian mage, Abramelin, to Abraham of Worms (c.1362-c.1458).

Crowley moved in and commenced a lengthy ritual for summoning one's Holy Guardian Angel, which required a preparation period of six months of celibacy an abstinence. At some point in the ritual, Crowley was called away. Allegedly, chaos erupted. A maid left, a workman went insane, and, by association, a butcher severed an artery and bled to death—Crowley had written the names of demons on his bill.

The house was in serious disrepair when Page bought it. He renovated it, but rarely stayed in it. He sold it in 1992. On December 23, 2015, Boleskine House went up in flames and was mostly destroyed. The cause of the fire, if it was known, was not released, but the blaze was believed to have started in the kitchen. The house was owned by a Dutch couple who used it for holidays.

Page also bought art works by Austin Osman Spare.

Many have speculated on the influence of occultism that went into Led Zeppelin music. The Zoso album, as the fourth Led Zeppelin album became known, featured the hit *Stairway to Heaven*. Page said he was attempting to fuse magic and music, "... the four musical elements of Led Zeppelin making a fifth is magic unto itself. That's the alchemical process."

Page embroidered the Zoso symbol or sigil and 666—the "number of the Beast," an association Crowley made for himself—on his stage clothes and amplifiers, claiming them to be talismanic magic. He had part of Crowley's Law of Thelema, "Do what thou wilt" written on the original vinyl pressing of the Zoso album. When asked about his involvement in magic, Page responded, "I don't really want to go on about my personal beliefs or my involvement in magic. I'm not interested in turning anyone on to anything that I'm turned onto. If people want to find things, they can find it for themselves."

The association with the Devil in music has been written about and accepted for generations, but of all the bands and musicians that have come and gone during the history of "devil music," none have achieved the fame of Led Zeppelin. Not surprisingly, religious conservatives have attempted to link devil pacts or worship to the music.

Are the entity Zozo and Page's Zoso symbol connected? Earlier in the book we mentioned that "zozo" is a word in the Basque language for crow or blackbird. Is it a coincidence that the only music project in which Jimmy Page used the Zoso symbol outside of the Zeppelin camp was on an album he recorded with the rock group named "The Black Crows?"

Crowley and other advanced occultists were known for changing certain letters of words to maximize their symbolic and numeric power, and believed that realignment of these letters could either conceal or unravel occult knowledge and mysteries. Page has never publically revealed the true meaning of his Zoso symbol/sigil, leaving fans and occultists to speculate. Among the interpretations that have circulated are that the Zoso sigil resembles the Latin root for eyes, or is a stylized 666—both a bit of a stretch, but satisfying to religious conservatives.

However, the sigil appears to have been taken from old texts on magic and astrology, and altered. Page's Zoso resembles a zoso sigil for the planet Saturn that dates to the twelfth-century alchemist Artephius. In 1557, the Italian mathematician and occultist Gerolamo (also spelled Girolamo) Cardano (1501-1576) included it in his book, *De rerum varietate*, which discusses physics, mechanics, cosmology, natural sciences, demonology, astronomy, and occult sciences. The sigil is found in the chapter *"Ars Magica Artefii et Mehinii"* ("The Magical Art of Artephius and Mehinius"). Interestingly, Cardano's book was placed on the forbidden reading list by the Vatican—although many such books shared that dubious honor. The symbol also appears in *Vocabulaire Infernal Manual Du Demonomane,* published in 1844, which probably repeated the material in Cardano's work.

SIGILLA autem fic:

Sol.

Luna.

Mars.

Mercw.

Iuppiter.

Venus.

Saturnus.

*Gerolamo Cardano's Zoso sigil for Saturn.*

It has been speculated that Page borrowed the sigil because Saturn rules his natal sign of Capricorn. Whatever his original intention, Page's occult interests have led some to draw the proverbial six degrees of separation between his Zoso glyph and Zozo.

There are, however, interesting connections between Saturn and Zozo, via the "mother all demons," Lilith, an alter ego of Zozo/Mama. Researcher Josh Allen provided us with this perspective:

> In medieval Jewish thought, Saturn was viewed as the star of evil that brings misfortune. In Zoharic tradition [the Zohar is the key Kabbalistic text dating to the thirteenth century], Saturn (Hebrew, *shabbeta'i*) is personified and feminized, and is equated with Lilith.

Saturn constitutes the quintessential anti-sabbath force. Thus, the word play *shabbeta'i* contains the words 'I Shabbat," meaning "no sabbath."

In numerology, Z and O both correspond to the number 7. The correlation of the seventh day (Saturday) with Saturn (the seventh planet) was initially recorded in the first century BCE by the Latin poet Tibullus, and soon became commonplace in the Greco-Roman world. The letter Z contains two inverted 7's in its structure.

Saturn is held to be in charge of famine, tragedy, poverty, destruction, illness, bodily injury, death, and sin. These astrological conceptions were largely absorbed into Zoharic literature, Saturn now becoming the demonic Lilith.

Gematria is an Assyro-Babylonian-Greek system of code and numerology, later adopted into Jewish culture, that assigns numerical value to a word or phrase in the belief that words or phrases with identical numerical values bear relation to each other. The common name I have come up with for Zozo using all three Hebrew, English, and simple Gematria systems is Lilith.

According to the book of Zohar, Lilith was the first wife of Adam who refused to be subservient to him and left. She returned as the serpent to tempt Eve with the forbidden fruit in paradise. Lilith ultimately became the wife of Samael ("chief of the satans" and "prince of the devils") and the mother of all demons.

As the mother of all demons, Lilith would be "common to all demons," and thus share a collective consciousness with them. This may especially manifest in Zozo sessions with the female attribute of the "Mama" entity.

The beneficient spirit that rules Saturn has a Z name—Zazel.

Given the craftiness of Zozo, and the evidence that demonic entities like to play games with humans, a name wrapped in layers of mysteries and clues is not out of the question.

# 16

## Advice and Recommendations

The Zozo Phenomenon shows no signs of slowing down, and will continue to generate problems for some board users. Critics of the spirit board advocate avoiding the board altogether, preaching that it is "bad" and will automatically create serious problems. That is not, and never has been, the case. The solution is not to campaign against all spirit board usage—people are always going to be attracted to make contact with the spirit world, and will continue to use spirit boards to do so.

We believe it is much better to help people become aware of how and why problems occur, so that they can take heed of the warning signs and avoid problems before they start.

### Using a spirit board

Spirit boards, like all spirit communication tools, should be treated with respect. They are devices for accessing the dead, spirits, and intelligences, not gaming devices. In earlier times, spirit communication was opened with ritual to ensure that the human body, mind, and spirit would be properly prepared. The same principles apply today. We don't need to don robes and act out elaborate rituals, but we do need to bring a mindfulness to a session.

The potential communicators on the other side of the board, whether they are discarnate humans or nonhuman entities, read and respond to the "vibration" of the board users. In esoteric terms, the "vibration" consists of the subtle spiritual energy that every person sends out with their consciousness, including their thoughts, intentions, emotions, and psychological state. The spiritual energy creates a kind of light, like a beacon, that gets the attention of presences. Fear, anger, depression, and emotional upset create a vastly different spiritual vibration and light than confidence, respect, happiness, and calmness do. Likewise, poor health, fatigue, and drug and alcohol use will affect communication as well.

Your "vibration" signature contains the accumulated effects of your lifetime, as well as current conditions.

Here is an example of how Zozo took advantage of a grieving woman trying to contact her deceased fiancé:

> Thank you so much for listening and being open minded. I've used the Ouija board since I was a child. I've never had any negative experiences except this one time. It was about eight or nine years ago. I was grieving my fiance and wanted to try to communicate with him, so I used the Ouija by myself.
>
> At first it seemed like I was communicating with him and the interaction had me in tears, but then the messages were strange and didn't sound like him. I asked if I was still talking with Ed (my fiance who passed), and the message was NO. I asked who was I now talking with and the planchette started doing a figure eight across the board. Then it kept spelling Z then O then Z then O for a few seconds. I never heard of Zozo, so didn't think much about what it was spelling.
>
> I asked what it wanted and it spelled out AM HERE and LET ME TAKE THE WHEEL. I didn't understand what that meant. I was getting a bit uncomfortable and was exhausted from crying so I said that I needed to go and

said goodbye and the board said GOODBYE. I thought nothing more on it, just thought I got some message that made no sense.

About three weeks later, I was driving and the steering wheel of my truck suddenly pulled hard to the right...pulled isn't the right word, it felt like invisible hands took control of the wheel and steered it to the right. Sounds crazy but that's what it felt like. My truck veered off the street towards the side of the road and my side mirror hit a tree causing the passenger window to shatter. I managed to wrestle the steering wheel back and put the truck back on the road. I was shaken but okay and took my truck in to be repaired. Mechanic said there was nothing wrong with it (other than needing a new mirror and window).

That was it, but to be honest, ever since I haven't had good luck and my life has steadily taken a down turn. I never put it all together until I saw something about Zozo and the Ouija (which kind of freaked me out but intrigued me). I've used the board since, alone and with people, and as always I cleanse the board and I haven't had another experience like that one. To be honest I didn't feel so much like it was threatening me but more like it was trying to prove to me that it was there, that it could do what it said in the message.

The condition of the woman's grief sent out a signal, and Zozo was able to latch on to the energy. Her depression was a factor; there may have been others that she did not elaborate, but would surface in an in-depth interview.

Some people have "thin boundaries" to the spirit world and are especially vulnerable to opportunistic entities. They may not know it until they engage in spirit communications or paranormal exploration. "There are certain people who are going to attract something negative no matter what the circumstances are," said John Zaffis. "Even people who are very innocent can fall victim. You have to be guarded and grounded. It's not the board per se, it's the individuals who use it."

In her book *The Spirits of Ouija: Four Decades of Communication*, Karen A. Dahlman notes:

> We need to prepare not only the physical space for a Ouija session, but most importantly, prepare our own internal space, our vibration, for a Ouija session. The internal space includes our mindset, our emotions, and our spiritual and physical needs. We need to make sure we are vibrating in alignment with our intentions for the session. Not only is it paramount to have positive intentions set for the communication, I can't stress enough how you must be prepared for this interaction emotionally, environmentally, and spiritually.

We find many cases, however, where the board users were experienced and proficient, yet still had negative encounters. When we have the opportunity to probe deeper into the circumstances, we often find underlying factors that have played a significant role—sometimes unconsciously.

In some of those cases, the individuals anticipated that something "evil" would show up. Karen told us:

> I believe that an energetic vibration, such as what many call "Zozo" can be drawn to oneself, not unlike any other archetypal influence. This is no different from drawing another type of archetypal influence to oneself, such as the Puer/Puella Eternal, the Eternal Boy/Girl complex. The syndrome of the man or woman who never grows up can be viewed as either positive or negative. Truly these archetypes are neutral. It's when we give them meaning, we tend to give our power over to this complex. Michael Jackson was a good example of the man who never wanted to grow up. He was the eternal boy or the Peter Pan of modern day. This syndrome was neither good nor bad until he allowed it to take over his life. The archetype didn't embody him. He embodied this archetype. Whether it's a conscious or unconscious choice to allow such influences, it's still constellated by a choice.
>
> Archetypal influences are just energetic blueprints inherent within the collective psyche of all human kind. It

is through aligning with these blueprints that we learn to constellate their influence upon our own behavior, beliefs, and actions.

Per my spirit guides, they feel that many if not most people vibrate at such a low level that their imaginations do most of the work. They come to assign more significance to their experiences to fit the narrative that best suits their superstition. Some people even possess a greater belief in all things evil than others who never have such of an encounter, although both groups of people have used a Ouija board; they have walked away with entirely different experiences.

When someone possesses a greater belief in all things evil, they are so easily possessed. They then believe that a priest or demonologist can only remove it from them, as that is how it works per the superstition they've been told. Nevertheless, this belief becomes real for them and thus, becomes their literal experience.

Karen described how an angry encounter she had with a person generated a Zozo experience with the board:

I had an experience once that I can recall when the planchette spelled out Z O Z O. Prior to this experience I had heard and read a little about this name. This was before there was as much hype as there is today on the internet about this character called Zozo demon.

Earlier that day, I had an incident with a psychic in person where our exchange was heated. After the incident I sat at the board with a partner and inquired what was the "dark energy" that was present during the earlier interaction, which we both mentioned feeling. That energy supposedly came forth during the board session and spelled Z O Z O and told me that it was a dark energy connected to this psychic. I didn't like the feel of this energy from earlier in the day and definitely didn't want to go back into that negative space, so I told it that it was not welcome in my communications, space or energy field and to leave. Not a problem. It did leave and there was not any more exchange or discourse beyond this session.

## Prepare the inner space

Your inner space can be prepared in a variety of ways. Meditation, prayer, and gentle breathing exercises stimulate the flow of the universal life force through the body and strengthen the aura, which is an energetic shield around us that blocks negative influences.

In *Ouija Gone Wild*, Rosemary and Rick Fisher found a set of instructions that accompanied a nineteenth-century dial plate called the *Telepathic Spirit Communicator*, one of the precursors of the spirit board. The advice is still sound for today:

> When sitting for investigation into the subject of Spirit Return, try to take all possible precautions against outside interference. Quietude is a valuable aid. Place the fingers of one or both hands lightly on the Board, and sit passively until movements take place. When that occurs, ask the unseen operators to try to spell out a name or message. Should your first attempts result in failure, do not get discouraged. A sit often requires a few sittings before the power can be sufficiently controlled to ensure reliable results. Take care that mistakes do not occur on your part and always remember that errors are quite possible on the part of the communicator. Spirits are only human beings, and do not possess more knowledge or goodness than they have acquired by their own efforts, and if any should try to impose upon you chasten them kindly. Ignorant spirits will sometimes attempt to flatter and deceive. Always exercise judgment and discretion concerning all messages received. Be kind and sympathetic towards your unseen communicators. They may need your friendship. To obtain the best results, maintain a tranquil condition of mind and cultivate a habit of sincerity and honesty. You should not sit more than an hour at a time, and not oftener than twice a week. Two persons can use the instrument by placing one hand each lightly upon the board. After a little practice the person sitting at the board may be blindfolded, a second person recording the messages.

## Choose participants carefully

The people who participate with you in a spirit communication session will have an effect on the results as well as you. Individuals who have been diagnosed with mental, emotional, behavioral, or psychological issues should not engage in any kind of spirit communications. Others not suitable are those fearful of, or convinced that, something evil will manifest. Drug and alcohol use are out.

We do not recommend board use in paranormal investigations, not because of the spirits, but because of the unpredictable behavior of people who believe the board to be bad. Those individuals will alter the quality of the session.

## Set sacred space and intention

The environment of board usage should be prepared and cleansed, which can be accomplished with incense, sage, candle burning, and prayer. Have a specific purpose for opening the board.

## Invoke spiritual protection

Use prayers to call in spiritual help and protection—whatever suits the participants.

## Do not ask risky or foolish questions

Avoid asking how and when anyone, including yourself, will die. You may invite an abusive response. However, any response, true or not, will be deeply troubling and set a chain reaction of anxieties in motion.

Many paranormal investigators are fond of asking spirits, "Are you angry at us? Do you want us to leave?" Predictably, they get a "yes" answer to both—but remain on the scene, pestering the spirit communicators with more questions.

## Pay attention to warning signs

Zozo will often announce itself by the planchette taking on a life of its own and moving in figure eights, or doing the "rainbow effect" of moving rapidly back and forth from the Z to the O. Any names given that start with Z, including the solo letter Z, are likely to be Zozo. Be aware of its other alter egos, especially Mama and Lily.

For some people, the appearance of a communicator who seems dangerous is thrilling, and they feel compelled to continue. "People know they should stop, but they keep going," said Robert Murch. "They get hooked."

If the warning signs appear, dismiss the communicators and stop board activity.

## Use discernment

Many people have a tendency to take as truth everything that purportedly comes from the dead or a spirit. Evaluate communications and the alleged sources. Ultimately, there are few, if any, ways to prove exactly who is on the other side of the communications. Nonetheless, you should not automatically take everything on board. If something sounds suspicious, there is a good reason for it.

## Do a firm closing

When the session is over, firmly close the door by announcing the end, giving thanks *if appropriate*, and instructing the communicators that they must now withdraw into their realm.

If for some reason you don't do a formal closing, will problems happen? In most cases, no. The withdrawal of your mental and emotional energy will close the door as well.

Anxiety and fear will leave the door open.

## Dealing with the negative

Sooner or later, everyone who pursues spirit contact runs into negativity. If you are in control of the session, you can dismiss the unwanted, close the door, and end interaction without ill effects. If board users are inexperienced and vulnerable, they are more likely to be adversely affected. They may give their power away to the communicators and allow them to have the upper hand. They may be overcome with anxiety, which invites many kinds of attachments. The most vulnerable of all are young people, especially teens and preteens, who lack the maturity and discernment necessary for dealing with the spirit world, and who are dealing with the anxieties of peer pressure, success, acceptance, and more.

If you have any reservations, concerns, or fears about using a talking board—do not proceed. Your underlying emotions will interfere in the process. Take responsibility for yourself.

## During a board session

If Zozo appears—or if any negative communicator shows up—resist the urge to give it free reign and tell it, with authority, to depart. It may be tempting to see what the entity will say or do, but the more you allow it to perform, the stronger becomes its attachment to the session. If it does not leave upon command, close the session. Take the planchette to GOODBYE, instruct the communicator to depart to its own domain, and wipe off the board.

You can start again, but if Zozo returns, shut down board usage altogether.

Prayer invocations for spiritual help—such as angels—are helpful. If an unpleasant energy lingers in the environment, clear it with a cleansing, such as incense or sage.

Avoid giving Zozo post-board energy by talking about it right away, especially in an energized, animated way. Spirits feed on human emotional energy. Let some time pass, and turn your attention to something else. This strengthens your mental barrier.

## After a board session

In some cases, unpleasant phenomena may manifest after a session has ended. Participants may feel watched, sense a heavy feel in the atmosphere, and feel physically and mentally affected. Poltergeist phenomena may erupt. There may be nightmares and dream invasion. The heaviness and sensation of being watched follow participants wherever they go.

Some suggestible board users may actually scare themselves into thinking they have an attachment. However, these circumstances can also indicate that a personal attachment has taken place.

Do not delay seeking outside help from experts, who include paranormal and demonology authorities; religious authorities; and alternative medicine practitioners. The latter in particular can assess damage that has been done to the aura, and repair it.

Zozo is resistant to exorcisms and remedial actions. "I have seen cases in which formal exorcism, deliverance, and prayer have not been successful in breaking this spirit," said John Zaffis. Repeated exorcisms may be necessary, combined with other therapies or remedies.

Many remedial actions such as house blessings and cleansings, amulets, salt, iron, holy water, and so on, may have only temporary effects, as illustrated in the following story:

My two friends and I gathered around a table in our art class. We drew the Kakki-san Ouija board with the English alphabet. We asked if anyone was there, and he said yes. We began asking questions to make sure it was real. We asked what one friend's last name was, and he [board communicator] spelled it correctly. We then asked what my favorite color was, and he answered, BLACK. He then began getting scary. He said he wanted another friend who was watching, as in, he liked him. We asked what he wanted from that person, and he said HIS SOUL. We asked what his name was, and he answered, ZOZO.

We then began asking him questions such as, "Have you been to Raven's house?" and he said, YES. He told us it hurts him when he enters my home. He said that two out of the three of us playing were pure, but that I was not. When asked why, he said his name again. We asked if my friends were protected from him, and he said yes. When asked how they were protected, and by whom, he answered, RAVEN. The friend whose soul he wanted asked if his aura and protective stone ring were hurting Zozo, and he said, YES.

When asked who was protecting me, he said a strange, demon-sounding name. Then, he said, JK HAHA. That was when I got really scared. My friends wanted to stop, but Zozo wouldn't let us. We kept trying, and finally, after quite a while, he left. But, we forgot to burn the paper board, in which case, it may come after us. I threw the pen we used away, and my friend spent the coin we used.

I have used salt, scripture, and prayer as a protection, and also used a protection spell, but I can feel him following me. It is an icy, malevolent presence, and I started having nightmares last night. I also saw a shadowy figure in my home, twice, while washing dishes, only out of the corner of my eye. It disappeared, but I think he is still there, waiting.

The success of remedies can depend a great deal on the circumstances of a particular case, including the internal state of the victims. They must realize that they must participate in the remedy as well, by using their will and resolve to push away the attachment. If there are factors in daily life that have contributed to vulnerability, attention must be given to resolving them. Counseling and medical treatment may be necessary.

In extreme cases, it is advisable to avoid board usage, and also other forms of spirit communication and paranormal activities. For some individuals, this is a temporary period. For others, it may be advisable to stay away from the paranormal altogether.

Darren has helped hundreds of people attempt to rid the negative effects of the Zozo Phenomenon in private correspondence with varying degrees of success. "The first step is recognizing you aren't alone," he emphasizes. "Each case is unique, but shows similarities regardless of beliefs. There does seem to be a common dark thread that connects the Zozo experiencers. Arming yourself with knowledge and understanding is paramount. You have to come to grips with your fear, and confront the entity, or it can cause a dirty laundry list of negative outcomes. Some cases have had luck with religious provocation. Others, not so much.

"Zozo is out there, and exists regardless of speculation or origin," Darren comments. "It's there every time I use a spirit board, so I no longer participate in sessions."

## In conclusion

Zozo has demonstrated time and time again its formidable power and ability to disrupt and even destroy. It does not manifest to provide entertainment—at least to human beings. Its purpose, as demonstrated by its behavior, is to create havoc wherever possible, which may be entertaining to Zozo.

We noted earlier that negative entities gain an advantage when people are frightened, and when they give over their own authority. The best way to be in charge is to study to acquire knowledge of the spirit world, have a daily or frequent spiritual practice that includes meditation, and to firmly end contact experiences that become hostile. Zozo relies on lack of knowledge, fear, and lack of boundaries.

One hallmark of dark spirits is that they shapeshift to confuse and maintain their edge. Zozo came to attention via the spirit board. We have shown that this entity pre-existed the spirit board, and it has probably engaged in a variety of tactics over the course of human history. There may come a time when it tires of spirit boards because its appearances will have become too predictable, and it will shapeshift to other forms and methods of interference. The same precautions apply to any type of engagement with the spirit realm.

# About the Authors

## Darren Evans

Darren is a paranormal survivor and investigator from Tulsa, Oklahoma, who coined the term "The Zozo Phenomenon" as a result of his experiences and paranormal research. Darren has been featured as himself in film and television appearances in his quest to educate and warn people regarding the dangers involved with spirit communication. Darren's website is www.zozophenomenonbook.com.

## Rosemary Ellen Guiley

Rosemary is a leading expert in the paranormal and metaphysical fields, an investigator, researcher, and author with more than sixty books published. She has worked fulltime in the field for more than thirty years. For more than a decade, she has pursued negative hauntings and attachments, and has done ground-breaking work on the Djinn.

Rosemary is a certified hypnotist and does past-life regression and dreamwork, as well as psychic consultations. Her radio show, *Strange Dimensions with Rosemary Ellen Guiley*, airs on the KGRA digital broadcasting network. She serves on the board of directors of the Dr. Edgar Mitchell Foundation for Research into Extraterrestrial Encounters, and is book review editor for the Academy for Spiritual and Consciousness Studies.

Other main areas of research are afterlife studies, spirit communications, entity contact experiences of all kinds, and transformation of consciousness.

In addition, Rosemary runs her own publishing and media company, Visionary Living, Inc. She lives in Connecticut. Her website is www.visionaryliving.com.

# Further Reading

Dahlman, Karen A. *The Spirits of Ouija: Four Decades of Communication.* San Clemente, CA: Creative Visions Publications, 2013.

Guiley, Rosemary Ellen. *The Djinn Connection: The Hidden Links Between Djinn, Shadow People, Extraterrestrials, Nephilim, Archons, Reptilians, and More.* New Milford, CT: Visionary Living, Inc., 2013.

Guiley, Rosemary Ellen, with Rick Fisher. *Ouija Gone Wild.* New Milford, CT: Visionary Living, Inc., 2012.

Noory, George, and Rosemary Ellen Guiley. *Talking to the Dead.* New York: Tor/Forge, 2011.

Made in the USA
Charleston, SC
02 June 2016